THE ORIGINAL BLACK PANTHER
The Life & Legacy of Jim Mitchell

By John Cosper

In memory of
J Michael Kenyon
Larry Matysik
Dale Pierce

FOREWORD

Anyone who knows me knows that I'm a huge comic book and superhero fan. Some people may simply attribute my love for superheroes to my connection to "super" strength, but for me there is much more to it. My affinity for superheroes is all about their continued sacrifice, loyalty and willingness to fight for others. This time-honored narrative presented through the lens of good versus evil is one that I stand by and is a tenant that has guided me throughout my powerlifting, Olympic weightlifting, strongman and professional wrestling career.

My love for comics was certainly heightened in February 2018 with the feature film release of *Black Panther*. It was a big one for me. As a youth in Silsbee, TX, I was a tremendous Black Panther fan, so as you can imagine, following T'Chella from the Marvel comic pages to the silver screen was a moment I'd long waited for. But, there was something greater. Not only did T'Chella look like me, but he also unabashedly embodied the characteristics I wanted to present to the world. For me, the Black Panther was the definition of a superhero.

In the Fall of 2018, my definition and understanding of the Black Panther shifted far beyond the global box office success of my on-screen hero. On a chilly, Saturday afternoon at a comic book convention in Louisville, KY, I met John Cosper, the author of this book, *The Original Black Panther: The Life & Legacy of Jim Mitchell*. At this Comic-Con, John passionately spoke to me about the real life, wrestling Black Panther, a gentleman by the name of Jim Mitchell, a rare, impressive man with a remarkable story steeped in wrestling history. A story, I sadly had never heard.

Looking back on my chance encounter with John in Louisville, I'm honestly embarrassed to say that as much as I do know my wrestling history, I was remiss in that I did not know the legacy and importance of Jim Mitchell. Mitchell was truly the

"Jackie Robinson" of professional wrestling and was a man who laid the groundwork for me to succeed as a wrestler.

As one of only five African-American wrestlers to hold a World's Heavyweight Professional Wrestling title, I now know that I owe a sincere debt of gratitude to Jim Mitchell. For Mitchell, the first African-American in the modern wrestling era to break the color barrier, wrestling against white opponents for major promotions across the United States was a tremendous triumph. With Mitchell's success across the country, barriers were broken and doors were opened for pro wrestlers who look like I do to engage, excel and earn an excellent living in an entertaining field we love.

What also amazes and impresses me about Mitchell is that he was able to succeed in pre-Civil Rights America. Of course, I'm not naïve enough to think that Mitchell didn't have his detractors and didn't run into major social and professional obstacles. But, to know that a Black man was able to travel the country, coast-to-coast, without major incidents and was able to build a brand name as a pro wrestler is inspiring. The stories presented in this book are universal tales of triumph and perseverance that go far beyond the squared circle. Mitchell's life mirrored that of the superheroes I read about and watched religiously. Mitchell not only carried himself with dignity and honor, but he also offered the sacrifice, loyalty and willingness to fight for others that I so admired about my superhero idols.

In the wrestling world, we often talk about guys being "over" with the fans, peers and promoters. In fact, as a wrestler, short of holding a major title, being "over" is truly the name of the game. Through *The Original Black Panther*, I learned and truly understood what it meant to be over. Not only did Mitchell chart his own path winning over fans, promoters and peers, but he also overcame so much to do it.

Whether you are a die-hard wrestling fan, a casual wrestling observer, or a novice to our business, I hope that you delve into this book with the ferocity and curiosity that Mitchell's story deserves. Mitchell's story is important and it's one that has made me a better person. *The Original Black Panther: The Life & Legacy of Jim Mitchell* is a story that made me proud to lace up my boots for more than twenty-three years and to do so as an African-American in this business. Jim Mitchell is my definition of a superhero.

Mark J. Henry
- US Olympian
- World Champion Strongman
- Two-time World Heavyweight Professional Wrestling Champion
- WWE Hall of Famer

Good Luck
From
The Black Panther

INTRODUCTION

The story you are about to read is one of the most remarkable tales of pro wrestling yet told. It is a tale that will transform the narrative about African Americans in the early days of professional wrestling and inspire all those who have a dream to do something great with their lives. The story of how this book came to be is an amazing one in itself. That story began in 2002, almost 100 years after Jim Mitchell was born.

It all started on a Saturday morning in Toledo, Ohio, when a man named Dave Marciniak and his long-time girlfriend decided to go out for breakfast. A few tables away sat a pair of women discussing a house that had just gone up for sale in an old estate district. The previous occupant had just passed away, and the bank was looking to unload the property quickly. Dave inquired about the house. The ladies told him the building had a solid foundation but was in need of a serious makeover. Flipping houses had long been a hobby for Dave, so after breakfast, he and his girlfriend drove over to 1020 Franklin Avenue.

"I walked around the house once," he told me over breakfast fifteen years later. "I didn't even take a look inside. I went to the bank and made them an offer." Without even setting foot inside, Dave bought the house for around twelve thousand dollars.

Once the paperwork was signed, the hard work began. The house was indeed in a state of disrepair. Old, dusty furniture and memories dating fifty to sixty years back filled every room. Water leakage had done a number on countless treasures hidden away in boxes.

This wasn't the first time Dave had gone into a home filled with someone else's life story, but the things he began to find in this particular house were unusual. There were posters for wrestling shows from Kentucky, Arizona, and Ohio. There were programs from countless more states and wrestling magazines. He found newspaper clippings, personal photos, publicity photos, and state wrestling licenses. There were boots. Nine and a half pairs to be exact. He found travel documents, personal letters, personal documents, and even a monogrammed set of suitcases all belonging to a man named Jim Mitchell.

He also found pipes.

Hundreds - no, thousands of smoking pipes. There were simple pipes, hand carved pipes, and pipes inlaid with gold. He found letters that corresponded to the pipes. He realized that he had stumbled onto a serious collector's treasure trove, a collection of rare and beautiful smoking pipes from around the world. Some he bought. Some were gifts from friends. Some were gifts from fans.

Dave and his girlfriend got on the Internet and searched for information about Jim Mitchell. It had been nearly 50 years since Mitchell was a full-time wrestler, and scarce little information could be found online at that time. They confirmed he had once been a professional wrestler and the owner of a store called the Black Panther Carry-Out on Dorr Street in Toledo. Seeing that he had been active in the wrestling game during the sport's golden age, it was clear Mitchell was someone who, although forgotten, had broken a lot of barriers as an African American.

Dave was never a wrestling fan himself, but he knew an opportunity when he saw one. He stopped discarding things at random and saved what he could, storing every wrestling and personal effect that had survived the years and the water carefully. One day, he thought, it might be worth something. Dave's girlfriend even went so far as to find and print out a list of wrestling memorabilia collectors, a list that included Dr. Bob Bryla, John Pantozzi, and Tom Burke, all now personal friends of mine. Any one of the three would have been eager to get his hands on this incredible find, but Dave never made contact with them. (Sorry, fellas!)

It was more than a decade later when I first read about the "Black Panther" Jim Mitchell for the first time. It was at the Louisville (Kentucky) Free Public Library in downtown, just a block away from the Spalding University Student Center, the building once known as the Columbia Gym, where fans used to go every

Tuesday night to watch the weekly wrestling card presented by the Allen Athletic Club. I was hard at work, researching the Allen Club era in the old *Courier-Journal* archives housed on microfilm on the second floor for my first book *Bluegrass Brawlers: The Story of Professional Wrestling in Louisville.*

Mitchell was one of four major African American stars who made a few stops in Louisville in the early 1940s, along with Seelie Samara, King Kong Clayton, and "Gentleman" Jack Claybourne. One particular write up indicated Mitchell was a Louisville native, a one-time bellboy at the Galt House hotel, who left town to travel the world and become a wrestling star. It was then that I became fascinated with Mitchell.

I sought out every source I could find on him. I befriended wrestling historians like Tom Burke and the late J Michael Kenyon who both shared with me everything they had on the subject. I read the story about the riot at the Olympic Auditorium for the first time in the book, *Whatever Happened to Gorgeous George?* I interviewed the few men I could find who knew him personally, including "Flying Fred" Curry and Dr. Jerry Graham, Jr. There still was not much to go on, but over the next few years, I continued to research the man and share what I learned in future books (*Louisville's Greatest Show*) and my blog.

The more I learned about him, the more I wanted to tell his story. I wanted to get him inducted into every major pro wrestling hall of fame and the Kentucky Athletic Hall of Fame. I created an outline for a book and wrote a handful of chapters, but I quickly got stuck. There were no surviving relatives to contact, and there was only so much information to be found. There wasn't enough information to warrant even a short book.

In the summer of 2017, one of Dave Marciniak's friends found my blog. He emailed me and told me about the memorabilia Dave had found in Mitchell's house. I called Dave on the day I made my first drive to the George Tragos/Lou Thesz Pro Wrestling Hall of Fame in Waterloo, Iowa. Dave agreed to meet with me, and two months later, I made the drive to Toledo.

Dave and I met for breakfast at Big Boy, and as we enjoyed the morning buffet, he told me the story I just told you. He told me about some of the unusual things he had found including photos with celebrities, a golf trophy, and the pipes. Dave had always wondered why a man who accomplished as much as Mitchell did had been lost to history.

An hour later we made the short drive to Dave's home, where the Panther's remaining personal effects were waiting for me in the living room. You know that scene in the Brendan Frasier *Mummy* movie where they move the mirror to light up the room, and all of the sudden, all the gold comes into view? It was sort of like that. There were the pipes. Lots, and lots, and lots of pipes. There were posters and programs and letters. There were famous faces and famous names on letterhead, program covers, and magazines. Within minutes, I had found the program from the Olympic Auditorium from August 24, 1949, the night of the riot, and a letter from the California State Athletic Commission, ordering Mitchell to appear before them and explain his part in the incident.

The story I had longed to tell had found me.

We spent several hours sitting on the floor of the living room, sorting the old papers and photos carefully. Dave's dog, a rescue he had recently adopted, bounced back and forth between the two of us. "He loves the smell of these old papers," Dave told me. I did too.

Dave had just recently retired, and his desire was to sell what he could at the best price he could get. We worked out an arrangement, and I loaded up my car with as much gold as would fit for that trip. I made a second trek to Toledo several months later to reload, taking everything except the pipes. We agreed that the pipes should stay together, and as of this printing, we are continuing to search for someone who will purchase and keep them together.

Over the course of the next year, we sold countless memories to wrestling collectors across the United States and even Japan. Dave paid me a commission on the sales, and I turned around and spent some of it on items I wanted to keep for myself (Sorry, Jessica). Every letter, photo, document, poster, and program was scanned, over 850 articles in all. Finally, after the last sale closed, I found the time to open my original manuscript, log on to newspapers.com, and begin the process of putting this story in print.

The lament of historians everywhere, no matter what their area of focus, is that too much of history ends up in the trash. Dave told me when we first met that due to water damage, he probably threw away twice as much as he was able to save. That said, it was nothing short of serendipity that led him to save what he did. Pro wrestling fans and history buffs owe him a debt that can never be repaid. This story would only be a small fragment without him.

It has been my honor and privilege to bring the story of "The Black Panther" Jim Mitchell to the modern world. My sincere thanks to Dave Marciniak for helping to make it possible!

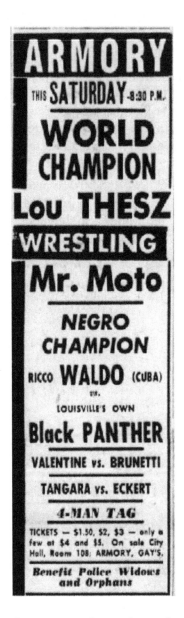

Louisville, Kentucky was proud to welcome hometown boy Jim Mitchell in 1954.

WELCOME HOME, JIM

The actual number of fans in attendance at the 1954 Police Benefit Show has been disputed by those who worked the Louisville Gardens (then known as the Jefferson County Armory) in the 1970s and 80s. The *Courier-Journal* reported the totals given to them by the Allen Athletic Club: 9055. The number was 329 less than the 1953 show, and according to Rip Rogers and Jim Cornette, still way too high to be believable. In the 1970s the maximum capacity of the building was well under 8000.

Regardless how many men and women packed into the Armory with its vaulted ceiling and giant steel arches (the drop ceiling now crumbling in the rafters of the abandoned building had not yet been installed), the atmosphere that night was akin to a family reunion. The Police Benefit Show, an annual event created by promoter Francis S. "Mac" McDonogh to raise money for the Widows and Orphans Fund for the Louisville Police Department, had become the Allen Athletic Club's biggest show of the year, featuring some of the biggest national stars in professional wrestling. After hosting West Coast superstar Baron Michele Leone a year earlier, the Allen Club welcomed Japanese sensation Mr. Moto to town for a main event against the world champion, Lou Thesz.

In 1954 Thesz had already established his legend as one of the greatest wrestlers of all time, but Thesz was no stranger to Louisville. In the early 40s Thesz began making appearances for the Allen Athletic Club, often being billed as Don Louis Thesz. For Thesz, and for many others in attendance at the Police Show, the event was a homecoming for those who had worked to make the promotion a Tuesday night tradition for nearly twenty years.

Founded in 1935 by promoter Heywood Allen, the Allen Athletic Club was purchased in 1947 by Allen's protégé Francis McDonogh and his wife Betty. Mac was a former sports writer, and Betty a former kindergarten teacher. Both were integral parts of the

15

company's first twelve years, and in the seven years since taking over, they had introduced live wrestling to the Louisville TV market, grown attendance, and created the Police Benefit show.

Ring announcer George Lewis, the voice of Louisville wrestling for more than two decades, was also on hand. Sergeant Buck Moore, a Louisville police officer who would later train a young recruit named Dean Hill (the voice of Louisville's Ohio Valley Wrestling), laced up the boots that night as he did every year for the police benefit show. Donning the stripes of a referee that night was Blacksmith Pedigo, a Glasgow, Kentucky native whose career stretched all the way back to the 1920s. It was Pedigo the *Courier-Journal* reporter was watching when another old timer, a local boy who had left town and made it big, walked in the room.

Wrestlers have long had a tradition when arriving for an event. Even today, every wrestler shakes hands with every other man and woman in the back, a sign of friendship and mutual respect. Pedigo didn't just shake hands with the man once known as the Black Panther. He walked up to his old friend and embraced him, slapping him on the back as only old friends will do.

It was a sight that would have shocked many of the fans in attendance, not because of the personalities involved but because of their skin color. Pedigo was white; Jim Mitchell, the Black Panther, was black. Had the two left the building and walked down the street to a restaurant, they would have been forced to sit apart, but the bond of brotherhood that forms between men in their unique line of work had long ago broken down barriers society refused to change.

On that night Mitchell squared off with another African American, his protégé and sometime tag team partner Ricky Waldo. Mitchell and Waldo were the "wind up" match, second to last before Thesz and Moto. The returning hometown hero took two out of three falls over his student.

As thrilling as it was to see one of their own welcomed and honored as a hometown hero that night, Louisville's African American community had a long road ahead in seeking equality. Several weeks after the Police Show, the Louisville neighborhood of Shively became the unlikely staging ground for a violent racial

16

stand-off. A group of white civil rights activists led by Carl and Ann Braden purchased a home in an all-white neighborhood and transferred ownership to the Wade family, an African American couple with a two-year-old and a baby on the way.

The very first night after the Wades moved in, they heard gunshots; their new neighbors were shooting at their new home. Andrew Wade got his wife and child to the ground, away from the windows. He snuck a peek and saw a cross burning on his lawn.

The Bradens and the Wades enlisted the help of other supporters of civil rights to stand guard over the home, but the violence continued. On June 27 as the Wades were coming home, their house was blown up by dynamite planted under their daughter's bedroom.

Surprisingly, the Bradens were brought up on charges of sedition and plotting to set off a race war in the neighborhood. Carl Braden was convicted and spent eight months in prison before a federal judge threw his conviction out. In time the efforts of people like the Bradens would be rewarded as the march for equality picked up steam. Change was coming, and as it often has, pro wrestling mirrored that change as it happened.

Two years after Mitchell made his triumphant return to Louisville, Bobo Brazil would wrestle at the 1956 Police Show. His opponent? Stu Gibson, a white wrestler and football hero from New Albany High School and the University of Louisville. Later that same year, Louisville would become the largest city yet to comply with the 1954 Supreme Court ruling *Brown vs. The Board of Education*, tearing down the social barriers between blacks and whites.

Most professional wrestling fans would be hard-pressed to tell you who Jim Mitchell was. The grappler spent almost three decades traveling the world, thrilling fans across North America, Europe, and Australia. He won titles and worked the main event from Boston, Massachusetts to Los Angeles, California, but his name, like too many, was lost to history due in part to the color of his skin.

A look back at wrestling in its heyday and the names that are remembered from that era might make you believe that non-white athletes simply weren't a part of the business prior to the 1960s, but African Americans were drawn to wrestling from the very beginning. The African-American wrestlers had fans the same as their white counterparts, and promoters, who were always looking to make that extra dollar, were more than happy to give the paying public what they wanted.

Mitchell earned his way into the business in the Midwest during the 1930s. After serving his country in World War II, he resumed his dream and made his way to the Los Angeles promotion that would break new ground for the professional wrestling on television and in the ring. He worked the Northeast, the Pacific Northwest, Canada, Hawaii, Australia, the Southwest, and many other territories before settling down and retiring in his adopted hometown of Toledo, Ohio.

More importantly, Mitchell blazed a trail for his contemporaries and his successors. While Bobo Brazil is traditionally given credit for breaking the color barrier inside the ring, Mitchell was wrestling against white wrestlers from the beginning. He feuded with some of the biggest and most colorful personalities of the day, including the biggest star of his era, Gorgeous George.

Those who knew him will tell you Jim Mitchell was no radical, but he was not afraid to stand up for himself. "He was a true gentleman," says Jerry Jaffe, who wrestled as Dr. Jerry Graham, Jr. "When Jim talked about traveling the South, dealing with Jim Crow laws, he was never bitter. But you could tell, he was not a man who took s—t from anyone."

Jim Mitchell was a star on equal par with his white contemporaries. He was a premiere athlete who could go to a ninety minute time limit draw with anyone. He sought equality with other men and he found it in one of the strangest and most unique of professions.

Mitchell did his fighting in the squared circle. He influenced people one at a time, earning the respect of the men who worked alongside him and the fans who paid to see him do battle. Mitchell taught people to judge a man on the basis of his talent and character and not his skin color. He changed their view of African Americans

18

one town at a time, one match at a time, one person at a time.

This is the story of a pioneer. It's the story of a boy who dreamed of becoming a wrestler. It's the story of how his dream helped to change the future and the dreams for everyone - wrestlers and non - who came after him.

There can only be one true first. Viro Small, aka Black Sam, was a former slave and the first African American to gain acceptance as a professional wrestler.

BLACK SAM

The story of Jim Mitchell is one that changes a lot of accepted wrestling history. Mitchell shatters the myth that a "color barrier" ever existed in professional wrestling other than in certain parts of the United States. He was a breakout star, a main event level wrestler from an early age who wrestled whites, tagged with whites, won championships, and even worked a little heel. But before we can tell Mitchell's story, we have to go back and acknowledge the man who did it all long before Bobo Brazil and long before Jim Mitchell. This is the story of the first African American professional wrestling star, "Black Sam."

Professional wrestling took hold in America in the wake of the Civil War. Wrestling proved to be a popular past time on both sides during the conflict, giving the soldiers a way to blow off steam, entertain themselves, and win or lose a little cash. One story handed down from those who were in attendance at Appomattox has Ulysses S. Grant apologizing to Robert E. Lee for the appearance of the Union camp when Lee arrived to formally surrender. "Sorry about the mess, Bob, we had rasslin' here last night."

The fever for wrestling grew after the war along with boxing and a new sport called baseball. By the late 1800s wrestling had become one of the nation's most popular spectator sports with men like William Muldoon, Clarence Whistler, Evan "The Strangler" Lewis, and Farmer Burns becoming well-known names from coast to coast. Wrestling took hold in the circuses as well, becoming a popular side show on the midway and foreshadowing the more colorful turns professional wrestling would take in the next century.

The majority of the serious grapplers in the early days were white men, many of them veterans from the war, but early on, an unlikely hero emerged from the most unlikely of places. His name was Viro Small, and he was born in Buford, South Carolina.

For the first eleven years of his life, Viro Small was a slave. His bondage ended with the end of the Civil War in 1865. For the first time in his life, Small, like many former slaves, dreamed of doing something bigger than working on a plantation, and he set his sights on the world of sport.

Small took up boxing in 1870. By 1874 he had also entered the world of professional wrestling. While there were many opportunists in the pro wrestling circuit at the time making money by hippodroming - staging matches with a pre-determined outcome in order to maximize profits at the box office and gambling tables - there were others, like Small, who engaged in the legitimate competitions pitting strength on strength.

Small worked hard to get ahead as a boxer and a wrestler. His training regimen included hauling kegs of beer and sauerkraut around New York City. All that hard work would pay off in 1881, when Small stepped in as a replacement to face white wrestler Mike Horogan.

Small was a last minute substitute for another wrestler, and he made the most of the opportunity. He lost the match to Horogan, but his speed and agility impressed the veteran grappler. Horogan offered to become Small's trainer, and Small agreed. He adopted the ring name "Black Sam" and followed Horogan on the New England wrestling circuit.

Small became the first African American to win a championship when he won the Vermont Collar and Elbow Championship. He held the belt on two separate occasions, and the title opened new doors for him to travel and earn a living. Between 1882 and 1892, he won 63 matches.

Small began taking on audience members, who would attempt to last a time limit against the champion. Many men accepted the challenge, but it was a rare opponent who was able to go the limit and win against a man of Small's skill.

Small also became a regular at a seedy bar in New York City known as the Bastille of the Bowery. Located in one of the worst and most dangerous areas of the city, the Bastille with its wild crowd and nasty reputation made the ECW Arena of the 1990s look like a tea party.

One night Small battled a wrestler named Billy McCallum to a draw. When the referee declared the no-contest, the two competitors got into a heated argument. Small walked away, but McCallum was so enraged, he went out later that evening looking for Small.

While Small slept that night, McCallum crept into his bedroom with a pistol and shot the sleeping man in the neck. By some miracle, Small survived the gunshot and lived to wrestle another day.

The last record of Viro Small wrestling is an 1892 newspaper article that mentions him as one of two men defeated by James J. Conlin, who was answering an open challenge from another wrestler named W.H. Quinn. Small is listed along with William Johnson, a man who laid claim to being the world's champion, and both opponents are held up as quality victories for Conlin in his quest to face Quinn for a winning purse of $500. This would put Small's wrestling days at 18 years and counting - no small feat for any man in any era of professional wrestling!

Perhaps more of Small's life story will come to light in the coming years, but even if we never learn the whole story, it's clear Viro Small was the first, the one true pioneer who first broke ground for men like Jim Mitchell, Bobo Brazil, Ron Simmons, Booker T, Dwayne "The Rock" Johnson, Mark Henry, and the Zulu prince, Huperfulagas.

Wait, who was that last guy??

An ad for the January 1, 1909 contest between the "Zulu" grappler Huperfulagas and a mighty bull chosen from the Louisville stockyards. The results of the contest were so anti-climactic, it wasn't until 50 years later the results made it into the Louisville *Courier-Journal.*

IT STARTED WITH A BULLY

On January 1, 1909, one of the most unusual wrestling matches in Louisville's history took place. In late December of 1908, the *Courier-Journal* announced that a man named Huperfulagas would wrestle on stage in downtown Louisville. Huperfulagas claimed to be royalty, the descendant of Zulu kings from Africa, and his chosen opponent for his one and only appearance in Louisville would be a live bull.

Huperfulagas assisted the promoters in picking his opponent from the Bourbon Stockyards on New Year's Day. Huperfulagas expressed no fear entering the match, proclaiming he would not be in the slightest danger, while the bull, he vowed, would not suffer more than "temporary discomfort."

Huperfulagas made his entrance in front of the New Year's Day crowd wearing traditional native Zulu attire "somewhat modified to meet the local ordinances." The results were not recorded by the newspapers, but after the Courier-Journal ran a story marking the 50th anniversary of the match in 1959, an eyewitness named H. D. Browning came forward to give the results from that fateful evening.

It seems that the fine physical specimen that Huperfulagas and his people selected from the stockyards was not quite the contender he was purported to be. Browning, a former Louisville police officer, was on duty the night of the match, and when the bull was led into the Coliseum at Fourth and A Streets, he appeared to be half-starved and not at all interested in the proceedings. The so-called Zulu prince spent 30 minutes twisting the hungry beast by the horns, trying to bring the creature down, but when Huperfulagas began bleeding from the nose, police stepped in and stopped the match.

"We led Huper to a chair and he nearly collapsed," said Browning. "The bull seemed more hungry than wild. If it had been wild, Huper would not have lasted three seconds." Given the anti-climactic finish to the build-up, it's no surprise the *Courier-Journal* opted to bury the story rather than share such a dismal result.

Jim Mitchell was just five months old when the infamous man versus bull match took place. He was born on July 31, 1908, the son of James Mitchell and Lena Biggers Mitchell. Young Jim Mitchell grew up in a city that was already coming down with a serious case of wrestling fever. As promoters William Barton, George Beuchel, and Heywood Allen began to establish themselves, they started booking some of the biggest names in the business for shows at the Buckingham Theater (later renamed the Savoy) and the Jefferson County Armory. The list of stars and champions who appeared in Louisville during Mitchell's childhood could fill a wing in the pro wrestling hall of fame: Stanislaus Zybszko, Wladek Zybszko, Charlie Cutler, Joe Stecher, Dr. B.F. Roller, Earl Caddock, and Ed "Strangler" Lewis, who first took on his famous moniker in Louisville.

Details about Mitchell's childhood are as far and few between, partly due to the fact that his "origin story" varied from one interview to another. When he did speak about his early life in Louisville, he talked about being the only child in a very, very poor family, so poor that he had to go to work at age eight to help provide for the family.

In a 1937 interview, Mitchell told a Santa Cruz, California news man that his entry into professional wrestling happened purely by chance. "It was an accident," he said, relaxing in a cushioned chair and puffing on a pipe. "You see, in school there was a boy who used to make life miserable for me. I was kind of timid as a kid, and he used to whale the daylights out of me."

"Timid?" asked the reporter, who knew the Mitchell to be anything but timid in the ring.

"Yes, sir - TIMID," he said. "Anyway, one day in the gym another fellow and I happened to be wrestling when the coach of our football team came by. Right then and there he advised me to become a wrestler. So I did.

"And the funny part of it - so help me - is that my opponent in the first professional match I ever had was that same kid who used to beat me up in school."

The Santa Cruz reporter asked Mitchell how the confrontation turned out. Mitchell answered with a smile.

"I got even - and how."

Mitchell told another version of the story to *The Sporting Globe* during his first tour of Australia in 1952. When the school bully began making his life miserable, Mitchell made his way to a local gym in Louisville where welterweight champion Jack Reynolds had set up shop. Reynolds was from Iowa, the youngest of seven sons. He trained with two of the early icons of the sport, Farmer Burns and Frank Gotch. He made his wrestling debut in 1910, and on January 8, 1914, he captured his first welterweight title by defeating Cyclone Parker in Idaho Falls.

Reynolds was a legitimate shooter, and he likely trained Mitchell the same way he was trained. He won the World Welterweight Championship multiple times and was a regular in Louisville in the 1920s and 1930s. He trained with Blacksmith Pedigo in Louisville, and it is believed that he trained Ohio wrestler Wilbur Finran, best known as Lord Patrick Lansdowne, the processor to haughty heels like Gorgeous George and Lord Leslie Carlton.

Reynolds was in many ways the opposite of the physically fit and health conscious Jim Mitchell. He drank, he smoked, and he hated to work out. In spite of his vices, he was and still is considered one of the very best wrestlers of his size in the history of the business.

His career nearly came to an end in 1934 when he was charged with second degree murder after a man died in a bar fight. Reynolds abruptly canceled all dates in order to fight the murder charge, and he was later acquitted. In spite of all his personal flaws, he was beloved by fans and colleagues. When Reynolds died in 1945 at the age of 51, Louisville promoter Heywood Allen proclaimed that Reynolds was to wrestling what Jack Dempsey was to boxing.

Mitchell knew Reynolds was training wrestlers, but at the

time, his interest was not in becoming a wrestler himself. He wanted revenge against the bully. He finally got up the courage to approach Reynolds and share his story, and the champ was happy to show Mitchell a maneuver that would bring the bully to submission - a head lock.

Young Jimmy Mitchell worked hard to master the hold, and when he was ready to take action, Reynolds suggested he invite the bully to settle the score in the ring at a real wrestling show. The bully, thinking Mitchell was out of his mind, gladly accepted, but Mitchell got even, "and how," and found his life's calling in the process.

The *Santa Cruz Evening News* interview puts Mitchell's first match against his former high school bully in 1924. Mitchell would have been only fifteen at the time, but age restrictions that prevented anyone under the age of eighteen were likely not in place. Truth be told, such restrictions have never stopped any teenager bound and determined to enter the business, so there's no reason to think Mitchell wasn't wrestling at such an early age.

Welterweight champion Jack Reynolds, the man who taught Jim
Mitchell to wrestle.

Dressed and ready to travel. A very dapper looking Jim Mitchell in 1931.

THE PANTHER IS BORN (1930-1932)

It's hard to determine exactly how fifteen-year-old trainee Jimmy Mitchell made his way into the ranks of full-time professional wrestlers. Mitchell told his story many times, and as evidenced by the two versions of events chronicled in the last chapter, the story tended to change. Many accounts have him dropping out of school in order to pursue his dream, riding his bike hundreds of miles for the promise of five dollar paydays when he was still just a teenager. Some accounts had him finishing school before he hopped on his bike, rode 118 miles, and earned his first pay day - a whopping five dollars.

Sometimes he claimed Louisville as his hometown. Other times it was Toledo. Sometimes, he became a native of Tennessee. In one of Sid Feder's wrestling books, Feder states that Mitchell was an orphan who ran away from his hometown of Boston, Massachusetts.

In an interview with the African-American publication *Our Sports*, Mitchell claimed that he had tried a number of sports before settling on wrestling, including tennis, baseball, football, boxing, and six-day bike races. This tale had Mitchell training to become a wrestler in Boston and soon after departing on a trip to Europe, where he wrestled in Paris and Greece.

Mitchell spoke about this European tour frequently throughout his wrestling career. The tour was said to have lasted up to 18 months. Mitchell claimed to have wrestled all over the continent, during which he defeated the Greek champion Johnny Jonatopole.

As unlikely as the story seems, there may be truth to it. After Mitchell's passing in 1996, his step-daughter Roberta Conn confirmed the tale to the *Toledo Blade*. Mitchell was 17 at the time the tour left for Europe, and according to Roberta, his mother gave him signed permission to travel.

Stateside, Mitchell's name first appears in the Louisville *Courier-Journal* in 1930. At that time Heywood Allen was the booker for the Keen Athletic Club, a wrestling promotion running shows at the Savoy Theater downtown. A former "circus wrecker" with connections to the vaudeville circuit and the boxing game, Allen first appeared in Louisville in the early 1910s working as a referee and is one of a number of men who took credit for giving Ed "Strangler" Lewis his famous name. Allen booked Mitchell against Wildcat Carter of New Albany, Indiana on July 3, 1930.

Mitchell had likely been working for Allen before the July date, just without a name or any notoriety. Donning white trunks and a pair of white boots, the 160-pound Mitchell wowed the fans with his quickness and athleticism. He was known only as "The Black and White." The July 3 match not only marks Mitchell's first publicized booking but his first under the nickname Black Panther.

"He was plenty green, too, back in those days but certainly not 'yellow.'" So said a *Courier-Journal* sports journalist prior to a 1939 return appearance by the Black Panther in his hometown. "Very smart, also, for a wrestler, but not the smart-alecky type like most beginners." Mitchell did not stay in Louisville long, but avid fans in the River City predicted big things for him. Suffice to say, Mitchell exceeded their wildest dreams.

Mitchell did not have to travel far to get his big break. He made in-roads with the Indianapolis promoter Jimmy McLemore, and by 1931 he had become a regular in the central Indiana territory. McLemore, brother of famed Dallas promoter Ed McLemore, was a colorful character, one of many to hail from the McLemore family tree. A native of San Antonio Texas, McLemore served in the Navy during World War I. He relocated to Indianapolis in 1928 and began practicing law in 1936.

Jimmy McLemore belonged to the Civic Theater of Indianapolis, the Columbia Club, and the Indiana State Bar Association. He was also an accomplished magician, who founded the Indianapolis chapter of the International Brotherhood of Magicians and became the international group's president in 1955.

"Magicians are average people who have a flair for showmanship and a love of people," McLemore told *The Indianapolis Star* in 1956. His could easily describe the type of man who becomes a professional wrestling promoter.

McLemore was said to be the man who took Mitchell on his European trek, where he competed in matches aboard cruise ships and on land in countries like Greece, Turkey, Romania, and Russia. It was a learning experience, a time when Mitchell was able to add a number of tricks and techniques to his arsenal - or so the story was told in the years to come.

Mitchell made his first recorded foray to Indianapolis in 1931 where he debuted against Al Cortez on April 21. He returned in the fall to face Al McKee of Terre Haute and Bobby Sampson of Los Angeles at Tomlinson Hall. Indianapolis is directly north of Louisville, just over 100 miles, and Mitchell claimed that he rode his bike to and from Indianapolis to make these early dates.

In February of 1932, *The Kokomo Tribune* announced Mitchell's debut in that town with great fanfare. Mitchell would be the first "colored" wrestler to ever wrestle in Kokomo when he appeared in the main event against the undefeated "Speedy" O'Neal. It was Jimmy McLemore who introduced him to the Kokomo, hyping Mitchell as a "baseball and basketball player, a physical director of the colored Louisville YMCA and a linguist who knows enough of a dozen languages to at least order ham and eggs."

Mitchell won the first fall in his debut match against Speedy O'Neal, but O'Neal dipped into his bag of dirty tricks after eating the first pinfall. O'Neal worked Mitchell over, building sympathy for the rookie with the Kokomo crowd. He took the second fall in 36 minutes and the deciding fall just two minutes later when he tossed Mitchell out of the ring on top of some empty seats, injuring the Black Panther and bringing the match to a sudden conclusion.

With O'Neal's heel tactics and Mitchell's brilliant work in the ring, the Kokomo fans were easily swayed into the Black Panther's corner. Mitchell requested and received a rematch on Thursday, February 11 in a no holds barred, two out of three falls battle. "I wouldn't have asked for a return match if I hadn't got hurt," Mitchell told *The Kokomo Tribune.* "It would have been a different ending."

A crowd of 600 people turned out for the rematch, and O'Neal and Mitchell did not disappoint. O'Neal countered Mitchell's "scientific wrestling" with more dirty tricks and stole the first fall, bringing the crowd to a fever pitch. Fans were solidly behind Mitchell as the second fall began, and the referee had to warn fans not to approach or enter the ring.

The intervention would not be necessary. This was going to be Mitchell's night. Mitchell took the second fall wrestling his way, and fans tossed their hats in the air when the Black Panther tied the match. After an intermission, Mitchell and O'Neal resumed the war. Both men went to work fast and furious, trying to outpace the other. It was O'Neal who brought the dirty tricks back into the bout, head butting Mitchell over and over and knocking his opponent to the canvas several times. The fans were on their feet when O'Neal went for one more head butt. Mitchell lowered his own head, and - CRACK! Both men staggered and fell to the mat. O'Neal was out, but Mitchell had just enough wherewithal to crawl over to his foe and cover him, taking the third fall and the victory as the fans let out a mighty cheer. The fans were thrilled to see the notorious Speedy O'Neal get what was coming to him, but Mitchell's victory was much more significant than the Kokomo crowd realized. Mitchell had won a main event contest against a white wrestler in 1932, and he was just 23 years old.

For many years it has been accepted as fact that it was Bobo Brazil who broke the "color barrier" in wrestling, opening the door for black men to wrestle against whites. The WWE, known world-wide for its unique form of revisionist history, has advanced this storyline no doubt due to Brazil's connections with promotion he knew as the WWWF, but it originated with the local press and promotion in Indianapolis under Balk Estes and Jim Barnett. According to Indianapolis wrestling historian Chris Parsons, it was they who originated the storyline that Brazil would be the first black to wrestle whites in the Indiana territory, despite the fact that Mitchell was doing the same more than two decades earlier. Brazil was the first black man to wrestle white grapplers on television, and that is most likely the reason such a myth was ever sold as fact to begin with - as if anything that happened before televised wrestling did not actually happen.

Mitchell wrestled a number of matches against African American rivals throughout his career, but the reality is when Mitchell started wrestling, there simply weren't enough black wrestlers working in the 1930s for a color barrier to exist. Jimmy McLemore deserves credit for pushing Mitchell in these mixed race contests, but the lion's share of the credit goes to Mitchell, whose talent and heart won over the fans and made him a star. It is a true testament to his skill and the respect he earned from the boys that he was already a main event talent by the age of 23.

A very early publicity photo. Mitchell was only 160 pounds when he started wrestling in the late 1920s.

Wrestling promoter and magic enthusiast Jimmy McLemore, who gave Mitchell a huge push in Indiana during the early 1930s.

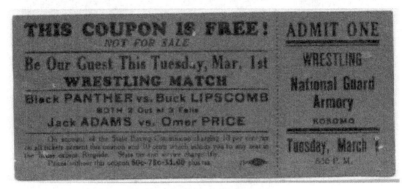

THIS COUPON IS FREE!
NOT FOR SALE

ADMIT ONE

Be Our Guest This Wednesday, Feb. 24

WRESTLING MATCH

BACK AT ARMORY 7th & Main

2 Good Bouts, including Black Panther Mitchell

JIMMIE McLEMORE, Promoter

WRESTLING

National Guard Armory

On account of the State Boxing Commission charging 10 per cent tax on all tickets present this coupon and 10 cents which admits you to any seat in the house except first 3 rows Gen'l Adm. State tax and service charge 10c. Prices without this coupon 50c-75c-$1.00 plus tax. 75

Wednesday, Feb. 24
8:30 P. M.

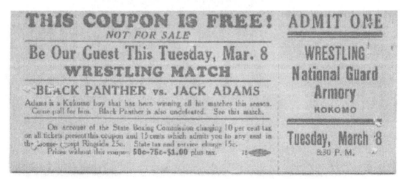

THIS COUPON IS FREE!
NOT FOR SALE

ADMIT ONE

Be Our Guest This Tuesday, Mar. 1st

WRESTLING MATCH

Black PANTHER vs. Buck LIPSCOMB
BOTH 2 Out of 3 Falls

Jack ADAMS vs. Omer PRICE

WRESTLING

National Guard Armory

KOKOMO

On account of the State Boxing Commission charging 10 per cent tax on all tickets present this coupon and 10 cents which admits you to any seat in the house except Ringside. State tax and service charge 10c. Prices without this coupon 50c-75c-$1.00 plus tax. 75

Tuesday, March 1
8:30 P. M.

THIS COUPON IS FREE!
NOT FOR SALE

ADMIT ONE

Be Our Guest This Tuesday, Mar. 8

WRESTLING MATCH

BLACK PANTHER vs. JACK ADAMS

Adams is a Kokomo boy that has been winning all his matches this season. Come pull for him. Black Panther is also undefeated. See this match.

WRESTLING

National Guard Armory

KOKOMO

On account of the State Boxing Commission charging 10 per cent tax on all tickets present this coupon and 15 cents which admits you to any seat in the house except Ringside 25c. State tax and service charge 15c. Prices without this coupon 50c-75c-$1.00 plus tax. 75

Tuesday, March 8
8:30 P. M.

A collection of wrestling tickets from Kokomo and Indianapolis, Indiana, 1932. Images courtesy of Chris Parsons.

Ticket 1

"DEPRESSION" COUPON!!

EXCHANGE AT BOX OFFICE

This Ticket and 25c will Admit One to Our Wrestling Show

Johnny CARLIN vs. Black PANTHER

Heading All Star Card   2 Out of 3 Falls—2 Hour Time Limit

THREE BIG BOUTS

national Guard Armory—Tues,, Mar, 22, 8:30 P.M.

Kokomo

Complimentary Ticket

▼

ADMIT ONE

▼

WEDNESDAY, MARCH 22, 1932

This ticket and 20c good for one regular 50c General Admission. This Ticket and 85c good for $1.00 Ringside.

Ticket 2

Popular Price Bargain Night!

EXCHANGE AT BOX OFFICE

This Ticket and 25c will Admit One to Our Wrestling Show

JOHNNY CARLIN vs. BLACK PANTHER

2 OUT OF 3 FALLS - 1 HOUR TIME LIMIT

Three Big Bouts

National Guard Armory—Wed., Apr. 27, 8:30 P. M.

ANDERSON

Complimentary Ticket

▼

ADMIT ONE

▼

WEDNESDAY, APRIL 27, 1932

This ticket and 25c good for one regular General Admission. This ticket and 50c good for Ringside.

Ticket 3

LOOK! What A WRESTLING Show!

Coach THOM vs. Swede Johnny CARLIN

Here Is A Bout Mate You Better Not Miss!

Merle DOLBY vs. Masked MARVEL

Black Panther Mitchell vs. Irish Pat McCarthy

2 Good Prelims   Biggest Card of Season—5 Bouts

On account of the State Boxing Commission charging 10 per cent tax on all tickets present this coupon and 20 cents which admits you to any general admission seat in the house. State tax and service charge 20c.

Prices without this coupon 50c-75c-$1.00 plus tax.

Bargain Coupon!

This Coupon and 20c Good for Gen. Adm. 40c for Best Ringside. 15c for Kids.

SHRINE TEMPLE

Terre Haute

Thursday, May 12

First Bout at 8:30

Ticket 4

Gala! Jubilee 200TH WEEK Anniversary!

"This week will be the 200th Wrestling Show I have offered my Indianapolis fans. Four years I have served you. Four years you have come to Tomlinson Hall. 8 weeks Broad Ripple to the Armory to patronize my matchmaking. This week leave your $1.00 at home. Bring a dime and be my guest." —Jimmie McLemore.

A Regular $1.00 to $2.00 Show —including the following Stars Bobby Chick, Stan West, Swede Carlin, Black Panther, Lee Umbles

On account of the State Boxing Commission charging 10 per cent tax on all tickets present this coupon and 10 cents which admits you to our general admission seat in the house. State tax and service charge 10c. Come early as these free seats will be crowded. However for 25c extra you may get more than unreserved admission. Ringside seats with this free ticket, 25c extra except first few rows.

Prices without this coupon 55c-85c-$1.10.

ADMIT ONE

ONE NIGHT ONLY

Fri. May 20th 8:30

This Ticket **FREE** NOT for Sale

ARMORY

Former Indiana University wrestler Buck Weaver. Mitchell and Weaver would battle one another for many years across the United States.

It's worth noting before we go further into his story that that Jim Mitchell was hardly the first nor the last wrestler to use the nickname, "Black Panther." In the early 1930s while Mitchell was beginning to make a name for himself, there were several athletes using the name Black Panther. In fact many sports reporters, who loved to use nicknames, used the "Black Panther" tag on any speedy, strong African American athlete no matter what their sport of choice. It makes wading through the hundreds of newspaper stories about Black Panthers in various sports a bit of a challenge.

Here's a quick catalog of some of the Black Panthers who were roaming the countryside during Jim Mitchell's heyday.

Harry Wills was an African American boxer considered one of the best of his time. He was a three-time "World Colored Heavyweight Champion," but despite his popularity, he was repeatedly denied the opportunity to fight Jack Dempsey for his world title.

Ralph Metcalfe was an Olympic track and field star who won two silver medals. He finished second to Eddie Tolan in 1932 and Jesse Owens at the Berlin Games in 1936. He later became a four-term Congressman in the U.S. House of Representatives from Illinois.

Feab S. Williams, better known as George Godfrey, was a disgraced boxer whose career was derailed when rumors spread he had taken a dive against Primo Carnera in 1930. Godfrey decided to make a career change in 1931 when he attempted to break in as a professional wrestler. Godrey was usually billed specifically as "The Black Panther of Leiperville."

"Black Panther" Jack Nelson was listed as being from Butte, Montana and Memphis, Tennessee. According to Wrestlingdata.com, he was actually born Leroy H. Clayton in

Cincinnati, Ohio and worked more commonly under the names Tiger Jack Nelson and King Kong Clayton. He was a good friend of Jim Mitchell thanks to their shared profession and their association with the Masons.

The Black Panther moniker would also be bestowed upon Jack Claybourne, a native of Missouri who rose to stardom in the Pacific Northwest and traveled the world. Claybourne was an occasional in-ring rival of Mitchell's, and he later became a popular star in Australia.

Seelie Samara, another outstanding African American wrestler of the era, was also given the "Black Panther" nickname from time to time. Samara was often billed as an African prince, but in reality he was 100% American, born and raised in South Carolina.

Alexis Kaffir, or Alex Kafner, was billed as the "famous" and "man-eating" Black Panther allegedly hailed from Egypt. Odds are good Kaffir was no more an Egyptian than Seelie Samara was an African prince. I know it's hard to believe, but sometimes wrestlers fabricate not only their names, but their city of origin. (Have you ever seen "Parts Unknown" on a map?)

Salee Halasee was a little person who worked with other little people in the 1950s as part of the "midget wrestling" craze. He feuded with Fuzzy Cupid, Little Beaver, Irish Johnny, and others and frequently used the nickname "Black Panther." Mitchell and Halasee worked a few matches together in California and became friends, so he likely had Mitchell's blessing to carry on the name in the midget ranks.

Another Black Panther rose up in 1961 working in Indianapolis for Balk Estes and also in Cincinnati. Although his identity is not known, Indianapolis historian Chris Parsons speculates he was part of Fred Kohler's crew in Chicago. He worked side by side with stars like the Crusher, Angelo Poffo, and Fritz von Erich.

The most high profile name to wear the "Black Panther" moniker in the early 1930s was a young man from Detroit named Joe Louis, who became one of the greatest boxers of all time. Louis made guest appearances on wrestling shows as a referee, including at least one match with Mitchell, and Louis and Mitchell became personal friends.

And then there was the "monster" version of the Black Panther, a 6'6", 270 pound masked man who has an interesting link of his own to Jim Mitchell's hometown. Managed by Count Rossi, this "Black Panther" ran roughshod over opponents in 1939 and 1940 on the West Coast until finally being unmasked.

The man under the hood was Wee Willie Davis, a giant in the ring who was best known for film appearances in movies like *Mighty Joe Young* and a winning run on the game show *The $64,000 Question*. Davis appeared on the popular program shortly before the infamous *Quiz Show* scandal broke, and he always insisted that his winnings on *The $64,000 Question* were won fair and square.

The masked "Black Panther" routine orchestrated by Rossi and Davis was a hit, a money-making gimmick that played all over the country. After Southern California, Davis and Rossi took the act to Louisiana, North Carolina, Florida, Iowa, Northern California, any place a promoter thought he could parlay the mask into big box office. It also spawned a copycat a few years later on the West Coast who went by the brilliantly original name of Black Panther Number Two.

In the late 1950s, Davis took his winnings from *The $64,000 Question* and moved to Louisville, Kentucky, to become a wrestling promoter, partnering with Betty McDonogh (wife of the late wrestling promoter Francis McDonogh) and later Dick the Bruiser to promote wrestling in Louisville. He later worked as a guard in the Jefferson County jail in the 1970s. He was also an engineer and partnered with fellow grappler Prince Ilaki Ibn Ali Hassan (aka Agisilaki Mihalakis) to invent the Glowmeter, and early version of a heads up display designed for cars.

Most of the Black Panthers were babyfaces. Some were heels. But only one was truly evil. This Black Panther's story came to light in *The Akron Beacon Journal* in 1949 under the headline "Italians Pay Back the Black Panther." The Black Panther in this story was not an athlete or even an American. Her name was Celeste di Porto, and five years earlier, she had earned a reputation as one of the favorite spies for the Third Reich.

Celeste made herself known to the Nazis during World War II after a bomb was set off on a Roman street, killing 32 Nazis. A virulent anti-Semite, Celeste offered her services, volunteering to betray the people of her own city by giving up Jewish community members for deportation. This Black Panther took a stroll one morning, greeting the individuals she had marked for death with a simple, "Good morning." In this manner, a hundred people were betrayed, arrested, and shipped off to concentrations camps, where most of them perished.

Celeste served a short jail sentence after the war and was released when she asked for her freedom to become a nun. She had been out of the public eye for three years when, inexplicably, she returned to the neighborhood where she had sentenced many of her neighbors to death.

Celeste di Porto made the news as a result of her fatal mistake - returning to the scene of the crime five years later. A young woman named Florina di Segni, a Jew whose brother died in a concentration camp, spotted di Porto in a cafe and approached her. "Have a drink with me, Celeste," she said.

Celeste was alarmed, and Florina left to spread the word that the notorious Black Panther had returned. A mob of survivors, women whose loved ones died because of Celeste di Porto's actions, attacked the notorious Black Panther on the street, nearly beating the woman to death before authorities could grab her and lock her in the safety of a jail cell.

The Black Panther of Italy has no connection whatsoever to professional wrestling, but her story is an intriguing one nonetheless.

Wee Willie Davis excluded, the "Black Panthers" of professional wrestling were men who broke into a sport and forged careers for themselves despite the racial barriers and prejudices of the day. Mitchell was not alone in facing such prejudice on the road, and he was not the only man to work his way up through the ranks wrestling white athletes. Godfrey, Kafner, Claybourne, Samara, Nelson, Halasee, and others were true pioneers whose stories should forever end the myth of an industry wide color barrier.

Boxing champion and Black Panther Harry Wills.

Alex Kafner, aka Alexis Kaffir, was known as the "man-eating" Black Panther.

Seelie Samara was known only briefly as the Black Panther. He became a main event star in his own right. Photo courtesy of Tom Burke.

Salee Halasee and the original Black Panther, Jim Mitchell.

Known as the Black Panther in the Pacific Northwest, Jack
Claybourne also went by the name "Gentleman" Jack Claybourne.

The Original Black Panther became personal friends with the most famous of Black Panthers, boxing champ Joe Louis.

In April Jim Mitchell supplanted "Black Panther" Jack Nelson in the Michigan territory when he made his debut against Iowan Carl Clark. Mitchell was introduced as being one of the "cleanest wrestling negroes" in the game, no doubt to set him up as a babyface before his arrival. Mitchell worked shows in Battle Creek, Lansing, and Detroit, facing many of the same white wrestlers he faced in the central Indiana shows. He was once again working opening matches when he arrived in Michigan, but by mid-1933 he had worked his way up the card just as he had in Indiana.

Mitchell had a heated feud with Les Fisbaugh. Fisbaugh was a cobbler by trade, or as one paper liked to put it, "the demon shoe cobbler." The papers described Fisbaugh as one of the dirtiest men in professional wrestling, so rough that he had been suspended twice for knocking out a referee. In one of their early bouts in Benton Harbor, Michigan, Fisbaugh's roughhouse tactics crossed the line enough that Commissioner Fred N. Bonine took away a pinfall awarded to Fisbaugh and gave it to Mitchell. The match was called before a second fall could be decided to allow time for a two hour main event, and Mitchell won by decision.

The controversial behavior of Fisbaugh and the actions of the Commissioner were enough to add fuel to the fire and propel Mitchell and Fisbaugh to the main event. Fisbaugh won the final bout between the two in front of a crowd of 1,200 in Saint Joseph, Michigan.

Mitchell's box office appeal was undeniable, and much ado was made about his debut in every new town he worked. In July of 1933 Mitchell appeared in a much hyped bout in Massillon, Ohio. *The Evening Independent* reported this as the first mixed race wrestling match in that town featuring Mitchell and Charlie Carr. The match ended in a disqualification when Carr refused to heed the referee's warnings to stop using choke holds and other illegal maneuvers on his opponent.

Buck Weaver was another regular opponent of Mitchell. A former standout athlete from Indiana University, Weaver and Mitchell battled in Indiana, Michigan, and Ohio. Mitchell had notable matches with other Midwestern stars including Indiana University wrestling coach Billy Thom and Kentucky boy Blacksmith Pedigo.

In July of 1933 in Sandusky, Ohio, Mitchell had one of his first in-ring confrontations with Martino Angelo. Mitchell and Angelo went to war for nearly thirty minutes before Angelo scored the first pinfall in what was scheduled to be a two out of three falls match. Mitchell did not get up after the first pinfall, remaining on the mat for some time. He was taken to the hospital and diagnosed with a concussion.

As always, wrestling fans, take this with a grain of salt. The people who could have verified this was a legitimate injury and not an angle are no longer with us.

The injury could very well have been set up as an excuse for Mitchell to miss some dates in which he had been double-booked. The August 23, 1933 edition of the Benton Harbor *News-Paladium* says Mitchell missed a show on August 22 because he was still recovering from an injury suffered in Ohio. Meanwhile in Ohio, *The Sandusky Register* reported that Mitchell wrestled Les Fisbaugh on August 22, losing two falls to one. You couldn't pull that off in the age of the Internet, but you could get away with it in 1933!

On September 11 Mitchell wrestled Joe Guenther on the undercard to a draw in Detroit, Michigan. The results from that show were reprinted in newspapers from Minneapolis to San Mateo, California. He continued to work in semi-main events and main events in Ohio and Michigan weekly working mostly against Buck Weaver and Charley Carr. He made his Akron, Ohio debut with much fanfare on October 13 against middleweight champion Gus Kallios. Kallios, a veteran at age 40, dominated the match with a number of holds for 32 minutes before finally pinning the Black Panther. Kallios won a rematch on November 7 in Grand Rapids, Michigan, and his victory was reported by newspapers in Utah,

Missouri, Oregon, and Montana. He finished the year in Ohio with a series of crowd pleasing bouts against Jack Kennedy.

In 1934 Mitchell began crossing the border to work for Maple Leaf Wrestling in Toronto. Mitchell worked with a number of wrestlers in Toronto during 1934, including Larry LaBelle, Bob Weaver, Martino Angelo, and Dan MacDonald. Most of his matches ended in a time limit draw, though he did record a victory over Dory Detton.

That same winter and spring, Mitchell was once again matched against the notorious Martino Angelo. Of all the men Mitchell faced in Ohio during his early years, Angelo was perhaps his greatest rival. Angelo was an Italian-American from Buffalo, New York and one of the greatest heels of his time. The two men would become close friends, retiring to the same city of Toledo where Angelo would become a wrestling promoter while Mitchell became a shop keeper but in the eyes of the fans who saw them in the 1930s, they were blood rivals.

Some first-hand memories of this feud were passed down to Jerry Jaffe, who became Angelo's protégé when he broke into the business many decades later.

"Everyone hated Martino," says Jaffe. "They hated him so much, that even the most unlikely crowds would side with Mitchell. One of the towns they worked in the 1930s was more or less the center of Ku Klux Klan in Ohio. It was an all-white town, an all-white crowd, and they knew just about everyone in the stands belonged to the Klan. Yet when Mitchell went up against Angelo, the people cheered for Mitchell! They hated Angelo so much, they were willing to cheer for a black man if they thought he had a chance to beat Angelo."

In Astoria, Ohio, one hot night, Angelo and Mitchell pulled off a feat that would be unthinkable today. "Angelo got Jim in a headlock. He held him in that headlock for 45 minutes. Every time Jim would try to get out of it, Angelo would grab his hair or his trunks and pull him back into a headlock.

"Forty five minutes into the match, Jim actually passed out from the heat. Angelo dropped Jim to the mat, and when the fans saw he was out, they charged the ring and rioted.

"Mitchell and Angelo always got a kick out of telling that story. Today, you couldn't do a headlock for 45 minutes. Fans would be booing you out of the building and chanting boring five minutes in!"

Angelo antagonized Mitchell in a number of matches, some ending in a crooked loss for Mitchell, others in disqualification, but Mitchell came out on top on June 16, 1934 when he hit Angelo with an airplane slam to take the third and deciding fall in the main event in Marion, Ohio.

Win, lose, or draw, the Panther's reputation as a solid wrestler and a babyface fans could believe in remained intact because of how he was booked. If Jim Mitchell lost, it was due to the shameful, dirty tactics of men like Les Fisbaugh, Martino Angelo, or Wild Red Berry. Mitchell's victories came most often through disqualification due to the same roughhouse tactics, but promoters always sensed the right time to put Mitchell over in a feud and give fans the payoff they wanted.

Mitchell also wrestled a number of time limit draws against other equals. These matches usually ended at one fall a piece with some going 60 or even 90 minutes. On more than one occasion these hour-long "Broadways" stole the show, with newspapers hailing the undercard match as being greater than the main event that followed.

While Mitchell remained largely in one region for most of the early 1930s, he had to wonder where he had come from at times. Some papers had him as coming from Terre Haute, Indiana while others inexplicably had him coming from Algeria. Despite the confusion, Mitchell fared better than some of his contemporaries in that papers always correctly identified him as Jim or Jimmie Mitchell. Martino Angelo was one of several grapplers who often morphed into some corruption of his first name like Martin, Martonio, or Martonino.

The fans really didn't care if he came from Algeria or Kentucky. Mitchell was a crowd pleaser, and fans flocked to see him. "Mitchell is one of the leading wrestlers of the day," read the wrestling preview in *The Sandusky Register* on January 4, 1935. "His knowledge of wrestling and intimate holds is excellent. He has worked out and perfected his famous shoulder butt that is regarded as one of the most dangerous holds in modern professional wrestling. [He also] has unusual speed."

Mitchell had a particularly brutal match with Wild Red Berry during this Ohio run in Akron on January 14, 1935. The *Akron Beacon Journal* reported that Berry was none too pleased to be working with Mitchell and let his feelings be known with some rough action in their two-out-of-three-falls confrontation. Berry slugged and bit Mitchell repeatedly during the first fall, claiming a pin within twelve minutes and thirty-two seconds. Mitchell came back and tied things up with a series of flying head butts after being tossed from the ring, but despite a valiant effort by Mitchell in the third fall, it was Berry who claimed victory with a "solid slug to the chin and a body press."

In February Mitchell faced Martino Angelo in Sandusky, Ohio in a title match for the "Junior Heavyweight Championship of Sandusky," an oddly specific belt referred to in *The Sandusky Register* in quotes. Mitchell was unusually aggressive in the bout, repeatedly stepping on Angelo's bare feet and even tossing Angelo out of the ring. He won the first fall to a rousing cheer, and Angelo drew a chorus of boos after taking the second.

Angelo went into his bag of dirty tricks for the third fall, throwing a handful of saw dust in Mitchell's face. He put his favorite hold, the hammerlock, on the Black Panther and continued to rub sawdust in his face. Mitchell finally turned the tide and won the match when he caught Angelo with a "French Savate," winning the title belt. (Yes, apparently, there was a belt!)

Savate is a French form of boxing developed in the 19th century that uses only feet to strike. Mitchell's title-winning kick most likely would have looked like an early form of a superkick or possibly a drop kick, which Mitchell was known to use.

As "champion" of Sandusky, Ohio, Mitchell entered a long program against Canadian Danny MacDonald. MacDonald was a freestyle Olympic wrestler who took the silver medal in the 1932 Olympics. He and Mitchell became a must-see attraction in 1935 battling to a 90 minute draw in their first confrontation. Mitchell retained the title in a rematch with a 58 minute victory over the Canadian, a barn burner that ended with both men lying knocked out on the mat. With the referee counting down, it was Mitchell who draped his arm over MacDonald to retain the title. They met once more at the end of the spring, and finally, MacDonald got the better of his adversary, winning the coveted Sandusky Junior Heavyweight Championship.

Mitchell had spent a great deal of time in the Midwest, and in the summer of 1935, it was time to explore new pastures. He headed Northeast to Massachusetts to do a four month stint for Paul Bowser. The Black Panther's billing became slightly confused in the new territory. In some places he was said to be from Ethiopia, while in others was announced as hailing from Louisville or even Detroit. Few of these matches were recorded, most of those ending in defeat or draw, but a Mitchell victory over Les Ryan in Portland, Maine in August appeared in newspapers coast to coast. He returned to the Midwest in the fall, finishing out the year in the friendly Ohio and Michigan territories.

BLACK PANTHER

Promotional still from 1933.

Martino Angelo, one of Mitchell's greatest rivals and closest friends.
Photo courtesy of Jerry Jaffe.

A promotional photo of Wild Red Berry and his son, from Jim Mitchell's personal collection.

WRESTLING

8:30 P. M.

TUESDAY NIGHT, FEBRUARY 28TH

Main Event
Cowboy Bobby Chick Vs. Jim Logas

Semi-Final
Dude Chick Vs. Frank Taylor

Opener
The Black Panther Vs. Ralph Dunkle

General Admission 44c; Reserved 60c
A Few Stage and Ringside 96c—Children 25c
Advance Sale Now Dowrey Hotel Cigar Stand

THE BLACK PANTHER

Monday, Feb. 26   8:15 P. M. SHARP

WRESTLING
MASONIC TEMPLE
Mustapha Pasha vs. Speedy Schaeffer
(Turkey)   (East St. Louis)

— SEMI-FINAL —
THE BLACK PANTHER vs. GORILLA POGI
(Louisville Ky.)   (Argentina)

— OPENER —
RAY RYAN vs. JOHN FELIX
(Los Angeles)   (Chicago)

— POPULAR PRICES —

| General Admission | 44c | Ringside Seats | 96c |
| Children Under 16 Years | | | 25c |

These Prices Include Tax. Tickets on Sale at Ralph's
Sport Shop, Main Cigar Store and Queen City Gym.

HARRY (SPEEDY) SCHAEFFLE

A pair of wrestling ads from Michigan - 1933 in Lansing (top) and
1934 in Battle Creek (bottom).

60

Les Fisbaugh, the demon shoe cobbler who later turned promoter.

Dangerous Danny McShain would do battle with Jim Mitchell for more than two decades across the US. Photo courtesy of Danny Daymon.

FROM BOSTON TO PORTLAND (1936-1938)

Mitchell was as over as any man in Ohio by the start of 1936. It didn't matter if he was in the main event, the mid-card, or the curtain jerker, he was a fan favorite. While previewing an upcoming match against a new opponent named Frankenstein Wolf, *The Akron Beacon Journal* put it this way:

"The popular Kentuckian doesn't have the top spot, that being given over to George Dusek... but it is safe to predict that most fans will attach as much significance to [Mitchell's] appearance here as though he were the headliner."

Mitchell was undefeated in Akron heading into 1936 when he ran into a rough and tumble heel named Paul "Tarzan" Orth. Always pushed as a squeaky clean babyface who played fair and abided by the rules, it was Mitchell's virtue that proved to be his undoing in front of 1100 fans. With the contest tied at one fall a piece, Mitchell paused to help the referee back to his feet after being knocked down. That moment of "gentlemanly" action was enough to give Orth the opportunity to strike and score the deciding pinfall.

Akron was also the place where Mitchell first encountered another man he would share locker rooms with for the next twenty years: Danny McShain. McShain was born in Little Rock, Arkansas, and made his debut in 1930 at the age of eighteen. He was a stiff worker who bragged about his in-ring injuries as a means to get himself over as a tough guy. He was also one of the earliest adopters of "blading," cutting his own forehead to get "juice" in matches. When McShain moved to the West Coast in the late 1940s he appeared in three movies, including a spotlight role in Danny Kaye's *The Inspector General* alongside Joe Blanchard.

McShain had relocated to Texas before his first visit to the Ohio territory and he was billed "Texas" Danny McShane when he wrestled Mitchell in Akron. McShain was the new baddie in town, so it was McShain who won their inaugural clash.

McShain would not stay in Ohio for long, but Mitchell's tenure in the Midwest was coming to a close as well. Mitchell headed back to the Northeast by summer, working in Boston and all throughout New England. What's notable about his return to Paul Bowser's territory is that many of his results were picked up and reprinted across the country. When Mitchell defeated "Cement" O'Neil on July 13 in Portland, Maine, the story was not only covered in all the Ohio and Michigan papers that had covered Mitchell in the past four years but in Des Moines, Iowa; Muncie, Indiana; Reno, Nevada; Medford, Oregon; Baltimore, Maryland; Alexandria, Louisiana; and Greenwood, Mississippi.

Mitchell was a hit in Boston, drawing comparisons to Ed "Strangler" Lewis from *The Boston Globe* for his headlock skills. As in Ohio it was often pointed out that he was the "negro" on the card, but everyone seemed to have a racial tag at that time. In many promotions of the time you could find people labeled as the Celt, the Indian, the Italian, the Canadian, the Mexican, the Russian, the Hindu, the Greek, the Turk, the Kraut, the Jap…

You get the idea.

It wasn't politically correct, but even in more modern times promoters rely on racial profiles and stereotypes to create characters. It was, after all, Vince McMahon, Sr., who turned Terry Bollea and Frank Goodish into the Irishmen Hulk Hogan and Bruiser Brody.

Mitchell made headlines again in August when he suffered a serious injury. Mitchell was wrestling against Chuck Montana when Montana tossed him out of the ring. Mitchell hit his head on a chair near ringside and had to be rushed to the hospital. Again, take these with a grain of salt. There's no better way to write a guy out of a program, allow him to take some time off, or allow him to work another territory short time than to have him get injured, but it seems unlikely this story would have been blasted across the country if it wasn't legitimate. Serious or not, Mitchell was back in action the following week.

On September 2 Mitchell faced Sylvester Balbo in Boston. The main event bout took place in front of a crowd of 4000, and the winner was promised a shot at the Junior Heavyweight

Championship. Despite a valiant effort, Mitchell lost two falls to three to Balbo, who used a flying scissors to seal the victory.

At some point during his stay in New England, Mitchell made a trip across the border to wrestle in Nova Scotia. One of the oldest documents to survive the years in Mitchell's house was an immigration card from Nova Scotia, stamped and dated September 24, 1936.

Mitchell returned to Ohio and Michigan in the fall, by way of both Louisville and Algeria, and the fans were thrilled to see him. He battled Marshall Carter to a draw in Battle Creek, Michigan on November 16, ninety minutes of grueling action. Time limits of ninety minute to two hours were typical during his Midwest runs, and it wasn't uncommon for Mitchell to go over an hour with whomever his opponent might be.

Mitchell faced Tetsura Higami in Sandusky, Ohio on December 8 in a "Japanese-style" match in which Higami and Mitchell were required to wear jiu-jitsu style shirts. Mitchell towered over the Japanese wrestler and dominated the first fall, taking Higami down with a dropkick and a series of shoulder butts, but things took a turn for the worst in the second. After another dropkick, the referee ruled that Mitchell could no longer use the move since it didn't fit the Japanese style. Mitchell tried his best to take Higami down for the second fall, including choking Higami with his own shirt, but Higami had a counter for every attack. Higami finally caught Mitchell in an arm hold that Mitchell could not break, and the match was even.

Mitchell tried to remove the shirt for the third fall, telling the official that the shirt was restricting his style, but the referee made him keep the shirt on. Mitchell tried to overpower Higami as he did at the beginning, but when Higami stepped aside to avoid a dive by Mitchell, the bigger man knocked himself out. Higami put Mitchell in a combination arm stretch and stranglehold to win the match.

Mitchell shared a story in interviews later in life about an incident that allegedly took place in Youngstown during 1937. Read and decide for yourself if there's any truth at all to this one.

Jack Dempsey was on hand for the show, acting as a guest referee, and Mitchell's parents, who were living in Youngstown, had come to see their baby boy wrestle for the first time. Mitchell was seriously injured during the match and had to be carried to the back.

Mitchell's mother stormed towards the locker room, demanding to see her son. Dempsey moved to block her path, trying to explain that she was not allowed in the locker room. "Sorry, Mrs. Mitchell, but you can't go in the room. The regulations —"

Dempsey didn't speak another word. Mitchell's mother let fly with a punch to the gut that doubled over the world champion. "You couldn't stop me seeing my boy," she told Dempsey as she stepped past him.

Like I said, decide for yourself how much is true.

Mitchell began 1937 in Ohio and Michigan, facing old, familiar foes like Martino Angelo and Buck Weaver as well as new faces like Walter "Sneeze" Achiu and roughhouse Texan Johnny LaRue (no relation to the Canadian SCTV icon). Mitchell met LaRue in Battle Creek, Michigan, where a colorful Greek promoter known as Farmer Nick held court and ran the wrestling shows at the Masonic Temple. Born Nicolas Arthur Kiricon in Athens, Greece on November 3, 1891, Nicolas immigrated to America in 1899 and began wrestling ten years later at the age of 18. He paused his wrestling career for a few years to serve his adopted country in World War I, but returned to the mat game and purchased a chicken farm that he ran with his wife Nettie. Competition forced him out of the farming business, but he soon found a new calling as a wrestling promoter.

Mitchell gave fans quite a scare on February 9, 1937, in Lima, Ohio, during a match with Sgt. Bob Kenaston. Tied at one fall a piece, the match came to an abrupt end when Jim Mitchell struck his neck on the edge of the ring apron and suffered what appeared to be a fairly severe injury. Mitchell was unconscious for twelve minutes, and later that evening, rumors began circulating that he had died. Mitchell was okay, and he returned home to Toledo that evening.

While Mitchell remained a fan favorite in Battle Creek, in some Ohio cities the Black Panther took a slightly darker path than in times gone by. No longer promoted as the up and up, squeaky clean babyface he once was, Mitchell began to work dirty, eliciting boos and jeers from the crowd.

For many years it was widely believed that Ernie Ladd was the first African American to work as a heel because in racially divided times, it would have been dangerous for a black man to invoke the anger of wrestling fans who believed everything they saw. Once again, the Black Panther shatters the myths of the past; he turned heel in Ohio in 1937.

Mitchell had a series of spirited matches with Buck Weaver in early 1937. Weaver, the former Indiana University wrestler, was as speedy as Mitchell with a flying tackle to match against Mitchell's flying dropkicks. Weaver was a skilled mat wrestler as well, and he was very popular with the fans. It had to feel unusual for Mitchell to draw the ire of fans when he used dirty play to steal the deciding fall against Weaver in Fremont, Ohio on April 16, 1937, but at the same time, it had to be liberating. Wrestlers by and large will tell you it's much more fun to work as a heel.

The heel run in Ohio for the "dirty but still fun to watch" Black Panther did not last long. There were new territories to be conquered, and in the spring of 1937 Mitchell made his way to Oregon. Mitchell appeared in Salem, Oregon on May 11 where he was billed as "The Original Black Panther" to distinguish him from Jack Claybourne, who had previously worked the territory using the Black Panther nickname. He defeated Tommy Tassia from Chicago in the opener that night. The following evening he participated in a six-man battle royal in Eugene, Oregon. A week after his debut, Mitchell wrestled top heel Scotty McDougall in the main event in Salem and won. One sports writer noted that Mitchell flipped McDougall in the air so high at one point, "his feet collided with the tin light reflector over the arena and set it swaying grotesquely."

Mitchell soon ran up against Sailor Moran, a villainous wrestler from New Orleans who was then the Middleweight Champion at the time. Moran protested Mitchell's status, saying the

Black Panther had not earned a title shot despite tossing Moran in a battle royal in addition to vanquishing other top notch challengers. Nevertheless, the stage was set for Mitchell to chase another title in a new territory after the local athletic commission "forced" Moran to accept the match.

A crowd of 2000 fans was on hand to watch the title match in Eugene, and the Panther was put up as a 5-3 favorite to win the title. After splitting the first two falls, the men battled for 18 minutes in a winner-take-all finish.

Unable to pin or submit the mighty Black Panther, Moran resorted to some foul play, tossing Mitchell out of the ring. The Black Panther crawled back in the ring, only to be tossed a second time, and then a third. Mitchell was "injured" when Moran threw him out for the third time, and Moran retained his title when the referee was forced to count out Mitchell.

Matches like this one allowed "The Original Black Panther" Jim Mitchell to set himself apart from "The Black Panther" Jack Claybourne. Promoter Herb Owen used the Panther in every spot on the card against old favorites and newcomers. Jim Mitchell was as popular there as in the Midwest, winning fans with his daring, his flying shoulder butts, and his dropkicks.

By the end of summer, Mitchell was sharing the locker room with some old friends in a new place - Southern California. Tarzan Orth and Danny McShain were both on the card in Los Angles when the Black Panther made his California debut, defeating Jimmy Goodrich in seventeen minutes. Mitchell worked weekly on a Southern California loop that included LA, Wilmington, Bakersfield, and Santa Rosa.

Mitchell had some sensational bouts that fall against Danny McShain, defeating his old rival and stealing the show on October 2 in Santa Rosa. They were soon battling it out for the World's Light Heavyweight Championship held by McShain, but Mitchell fell short in his attempt to claim the title. He finished his run with some show-stopping matches against Marshall Carter, Bobby Roberts, and Wild Red Berry.

With Christmas approaching, the Black Panther surprised

and delighted fans in his old stomping grounds when he returned to Ohio for the holiday. Newspapers from Fremont to Sandusky to Akron hailed the return of the "Black Panther from Terre Haute, Indiana" (or in some cities, Algeria) with promises that he would once again figure prominently in the Midwestern wrestling scene in 1938. His slight heel turn from a year before was forgotten and forgiven, and his status as a fan favorite was quickly restored.

By 1938 Mitchell's former in-ring rival Les Fisbaugh, the demon cobbler from the East, was now the promoter in Fremont, Ohio, running shows at the Jackson Hotel Arena. Mitchell won his first four matches straight in his return to the city before falling to West Virginia wrestler Buddy Knox.

Mitchell faced "Bulgarian" Wrestler Steve Nenoff in an action-packed main event in Sandusky on February 15. Mrs. Ethel Morris, wife of Dan Morris, was the promoter of note in Sandusky and the lady who booked the weekly wrestling programs. The Black Panther and Nenoff split the first two falls, and Nenoff, with a dangerous Indian death lock, looked well on his way to winning the final fall. Mitchell broke out of the death lock, only to get pulled back in. That's when Mitchell surprised Nenoff and the fans by rolling his confident opponent onto his back and onto his shoulders. The referee counted three on the man who had the submission hold locked in place, but it was Mitchell whose hand was raised in victory.

On March 28 Jim Mitchell crossed paths with Wild Bill Simovich, better known as Wild Bill Sim, in Marion, Ohio. Just as Mitchell was often billed from strange locales (in this case Algeria), his fellow Midwesterner Wild Bill was listed as a native of Nicaragua. Wild Bill lost on a disqualification after only three minutes, tossing both Mitchell and the referee out of the ring and refusing to let them re-enter. In the words of a very poetic *Marion Star* sports writer, "The temperamental Nicaraguan, after being disqualified while standing at ringside, upset and flung helter-skelter a vendor's tray of popcorn. He vehemently proclaimed his prowess and in no uncertain terms dared anyone who had the inclination to step up and mix things with him."

Mitchell had another new rival during this run in Gil

LaCross. LaCross was a dirty, no-good heel from New Hampshire whose underhanded tactics had cost him as many matches as they had gained him. Mitchell was the perfect opponent for LaCross, a babyface the fans adored who could go to a 60 or 90 minute time limit. Mitchell also found himself squaring off against old rival Johnny Larue, the roughhouse Texan, and Hoosier star Buck Weaver.

Tempers flared in Fremont that summer when a bout between Mitchell and Texan Ray Ryan ended in a draw. Ryan ignored the referee's decision and the final bell, dishing out some more punishment on his opponent to the consternation of the fans. Mitchell demanded and received a rematch, a "grudge match" to settle the score the following week.

Ryan dominated the first fall of the grudge match on August 6, pounding Mitchell for a solid 25 minutes until he secured the first fall. Mitchell, known more for his "scientific" skill and his "clean" reputation, showed the fans that he could get down in the mud with the best of them. He dished out as much as Ryan had dished in the first fall and then some, winning the second pin with a hard blow to Ryan's jaw. Mitchell sealed the deal and won the third pitfall with a reverse crab-hold.

Mitchell faced another new challenger on October 25 in Swede Carlson, winning the match by disqualification. Carlson was billed from Green Bay, Wisconsin, but in reality was California boy Leo Whippern, better known to the wrestling world in his early days as Tug Carlson. An artistic prodigy as a child, Whippern was the youngest person ever admitted to the prestigious San Francisco School for the Arts, now the San Francisco Art Institute. He was a solid athlete and one of the dirtiest players in the game. As Tug Carlson, Whippern made a respectable living as a professional wrestler, but it wasn't until the 1950s when he became the nefarious Lord Leslie Carlton that his career truly caught fire.

On November 22, Mitchell wrestled against "The Man With 1000 Faces," Lon Chaney. Chaney, a Hoosier, was no relation to the movie icons Lon Chaney or Lon Chaney, Jr., but thousands of miles from Hollywood, Chaney did not let his lack of connection stop him from making a name for himself off theirs. Mitchell and Chaney opened the show that evening on a card that also featured the women's world champion Mildred Burke, defending her title against Babe Gordon.

Mitchell suffered an injury in Toledo in December, bringing 1938 to an early end, but by January, 1939, he was ready to get back at it.

(SECOND CLASS)
IMMIGRATION IDENTIFICATION CARD
This card must be shown to the Examining Officer at Port of Arrival.

Name of passenger   Mr Jas Mitchell.

Name of ship   NOVA SCOTIA

Name appears on Return, sheet   1   line   15

Medical Examination Stamp   Civil Examination Stamp

(see back)

(SECOND CLASS)
IMMIGRATION IDENTIFICATION CARD
This card must be shown to the Examining Officer at Port of Arrival.

Name of passenger   Mitchell   James

Name of ship

Name appears on Return, sheet   line   2

Medical Examination Stamp   Civil Examination Stamp

IMMIGRATION AGENCY
OCT 15 1936
HALIFAX, N.S.

ADMITTED
Non-Immigrant

(see back)

Jim Mitchell's Immigration ID card from his 1936 trip to Nova Scotia.

Personal photos from 1937. Mitchell's love for golf and pipe
smoking are already on display.

— WRESTLING —

Masonic Temple - Monday, Feb. 8

—Main Event—

Martonio
Angelo

vs.

Black
Panther

— DOUBLE SEMI-FINAL —

BUCK ESTES
vs.
DAN CADY

DICKIE GERBER vs. DAVIE REYNOLDS

ADMISSION
General Admission 44c - Ringside 84c - Main Floor Reserved 60c

Martin Angelo vs. the Black Panther in Battle Creek, Michigan.
February 8, 1937.

Newspaper ad from Oregon, July of 1937.

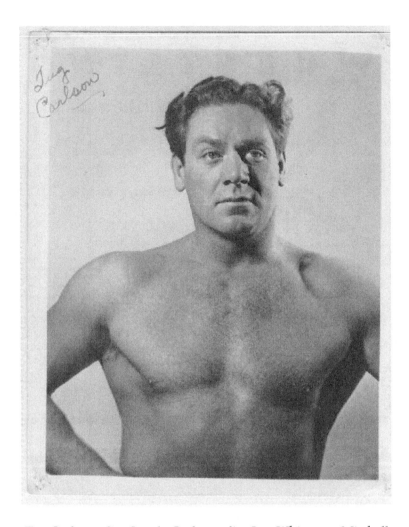

Tug Carlson, alias Swede Carlson, alias Leo Whippern. Mitchell wrestled with the Aristocrat of the Mat before and after his transformation into Lord Leslie Carlton. Photo courtesy of K.K. Herzbrun.

THE SPARE RIBS KING OF TOLEDO (1939 - 1941)

On January 6, 1939, Jim Mitchell added another first to his career: his first team match, and the first such match in Fremont, Ohio. It's hard for 21st century fans to imagine wrestling without tag teams and tag team matches, but in the 1930s it was something new and exciting.

Mitchell was paired with the seven-foot tall Billy Hall against Ray Ryan and Buddy Chick. Mitchell and Hall made for an odd pairing with their height disparity, but that was the tip of the iceberg as far as what made this match unique. To begin with, this was a teams match, not a TAG team match, meaning all four men would be in the ring at the same time. The heroes and villains paired up to do one on one combat, with teammates leaving their battered foe to come and lend aid to their partner when possible. It was chaotic, especially compared to today's tag matches, but there was never a dull moment for the fans.

The first fall was awarded to Mitchell and Hall after their opponents quit. Buddy Chick was no fan favorite in Fremont, and when he was tossed from the ring, a female fan sitting at ringside took a swipe at him. Chick threw a kick her way that did not connect but was enough to send the fans into a fury. A non-uniform police officer and arena personnel had their hands full calming the fans while Chick and Ryan escaped to the back. The first fall went to the heroes by default.

Things went from bad to worse for the villains during the second fall. The two-on-two battle went down to the mat, and everyone attempted to put a submission hold on an opponent. Unfortunately for Buddy Chick, his partner Ray Ryan locked a toe hold on him by mistake, thinking he had Hall by the leg. The error led to a falling out and the departure of Chick, who took a boot to the back from Ryan on his way out of the ring.

Chick's early exit left Ryan to make, in the words of the

press, "Custer's Last Stand." Ryan fought valiantly, but he stood no chance against the speedy Black Panther and his giant partner. Hall put Ryan in a headlock, Mitchell put him in a leg lock, and Ryan surrendered quickly.

On January 31, Mitchell competed in a five man battle royal with Martino Angelo, Dale Haddock, Sammy Kohen, and Dick Sampson with a unique set of stipulations. The first man eliminated was done for the night. The next two eliminated would be the mid-card match, and the last two the main event. Kohen was eliminated first, lasting only a minute. Mitchell was eliminated next, largely due to the dirty play of Angelo. Angelo was third man out, so the two found themselves paired in the following match.

Mitchell won the first fall of the singles match when Angelo was disqualified for rough actions. Angelo left Mitchell with a badly bruised leg, and when Mitchell was unable to continue, he had to forfeit the ultimate victory to his nemesis.

In March Jim Mitchell became the first man to tackle Mr. X, a new "mystery man" masked wrestler in Marion, Ohio, trained by the Masked Terror. Masked men were extremely popular draws at the box office during the era. When a masked man came into a territory, he would run down one babyface after another with his heel tactics. After two or three victories, the masked man became a hot ticket. Not only did the fans want to see him unmasked, they wanted to see him get the beating that was coming to him!

A popular star like Mitchell was the perfect opponent to launch a new masked man in a territory. Mr. X did not disappoint. *The Marion Star* reported that he "relied on everything that isn't in the books to score the win." Mr. X lost the first fall by decision after tossing Mitchell through the ropes. He then proceeded to score the second and third falls, solidifying his place as the new bully of the Marion Steam Shovel Arena. After terrorizing wrestlers and fans Mr. X was later revealed to be Buck Lipscomb from Indianapolis. Fellow Hoosier Buck Weaver did the honors in unmasking the mystery man.

Mitchell made a rare appearance at home in April when he finally crossed paths with Jack Claybourne in Louisville. Claybourne was working Wisconsin in early 1939, and the two had overlapped territories a few times, causing some confusion among fans who would arrive expecting to see one Black Panther but instead seeing an unfamiliar face. Louisville promoter Heywood Allen, now of his own Allen Athletic Club, eliminated any chance for confusion by pitting the Black Panther against "Gentleman" Jack Claybourne. Allen had a penchant for changing the names of established wrestlers who came into his territory, as evidenced by the long run of one "Don Louis Thesz" in Louisville. Mitchell was billed as the world's negro light-heavyweight champion, a title likely invented and bestowed on him by Heywood Allen himself.

It is interesting to note that Mitchell's hometown was one of the very few places where he was never booked against a white wrestler. Kentucky was a border state during the Civil War, and racial tension has always been an issue in the River City. It was also one of the southernmost points Mitchell ever worked. African American stars like Mitchell, Claybourne, and Seelie Samara always drew well in Louisville, but until Bobo Brazil's arrival in 1955, they remained segregated in the ring.

Mitchell and his African American contemporaries faced plenty of prejudice in the world outside the arena. Local ordinances and "whites only" signs often prevented them from dining, traveling, or staying in the same places as their white contemporaries. That said, when Mitchell stepped into the confines of the locker room, he was simply one of the boys, shaking hands with men of all races and colors every night the same as everyone else.

While activists, religious leaders, and politicians fought the good fight on the national stage, men like Jim Mitchell tore down the bricks by their hard work and determined spirit. They won over promoters by drawing in the fans, and they won over their fellow grapplers thanks to their work in the ring. One by one, the African American wrestlers won over the locker room until their white counterparts were willing to take risks for them inside the arena.

That's not to say that racism and prejudice did not exist in the locker room during Mitchell's day, but the boys in the locker room who might have had a problem with a man's skin color were nonetheless unified with Mitchell and the others against a common enemy - the man who paid them at the end of the night. Wrestlers then as now were independent contractors, and whites and non-whites were unified in their desire to get a fair and honest pay out from the often shady promoters after the matches.

Mitchell worked two more dates in Louisville with Claybourne in August and September of that same year. He also worked a few shows with another African American named Rufus Jones in Michigan and Ohio. Jack Claybourne appeared on several Ohio shows with Mitchell, not as an opponent but as singles competitors each facing different opposition. It's sad to think that decades later, many regional promoters, especially in the south, would have been reluctant to place more than one African American on the card.

By the late 1930s there were more African Americans working in the business. Still, no color barrier fell to divide Mitchell from his usual competition. He gave champion Billy Weidner a scare in a title bout and had a series of main event matches with native Ohio wrestler Stacey Hall that summer. Mitchell also faced some stiff competition from the Great Mephisto, a new masked "mystery man" traveling in the region.

On November 21 Mitchell was paired with Martino Angelo in Akron for a two-out-of-three falls main event with a 90 minute time limit. Their rivalry was a guaranteed hit at the box office in the Ohio territory, as hyped by *The Akron Beacon Journal*. "Angelo has been clamping his painful hammerlocks on the Panther for years now and the Louisville sensation has made the Italian howl with pain when he used his shoulder whips and whirling scissors on him."

The arch-rivals only went half the allotted time that night, with Mitchell winning in straight falls. The Black Panther won the first fall with a Japanese choker after 16 minutes and 42 seconds, and Angelo lost the second fall by disqualification when he refused to let loose of an illegal double crab hold, a hold very similar to the Walls of Jericho.

Mitchell began 1940 by winning a battle royal against Martino Angelo and several other regulars in Sandusky, Ohio. It was a much different match than the one promoted, as the star

80

attraction was unable to make it in time for the show. A car accident prevented Roy Welch from arriving in Sandusky in time for his pride and joy, Ginger the Wrestling Bear, to compete in the battle royal.

Later that same week, Mitchell traveled to Fremont, Ohio, where he faced a dark-haired Texan named George Wagner for the first time. The much ballyhooed newcomer split the first two falls with Mitchell before losing the final fall to the veteran Black Panther.

A month later, the two met again in Fremont. Mitchell won the first fall as before, but this time, Wagner took the second and third falls to even the score. Fans were impressed with the speed and the action in both matches in what proved to be a prelude of things to come. By the end of the decade, Jim Mitchell and George Wagner would become one of the hottest tickets in wrestling after Wagner would make a dramatic transformation into Gorgeous George.

Mitchell would depart from Ohio shortly after these early encounters with George Wagner for the state where the two of them would stage their greatest battles, California. A year earlier, the masked "Black Panther" (Wee Willie Davis) and his manager were one of the top heel attractions on the West Coast, but with Davis and Count Rossi now working Louisiana, the original Black Panther moved in to make his mark.

Mitchell began working a circuit that included Wilmington, Bakersfield, and Santa Cruz, working alongside old friend and rival Buck Weaver as well as California stars like Yukon Jake Jackson and Leroy McGuirk. In May he made an appearance in Los Angeles, where he once again shared a locker room with Danny McShain and George Wagner.

Later that same month the Panther headed north to Oregon. Mitchell made an open challenge in advance of his move into the territory, announcing he would take on all comers on the coast. Many fans remembered Mitchell from his previous run in the territory, and anticipation for his arrival was high. He worked in Medford, Klamath Falls, Eugene, and Salem against men like Bulldog (aka Yukon Jake) Jackson, Al Fcrona, Price Selaki Mehalikis, and the deaf mute Silent Rattan. Jackson was an especially good foe for Mitchell, being of the dirty, roughhouse school of wrestling and Mitchell being the "clean" and "clever" type who plays by the book.

In June, Mitchell suffered a shockingly quick defeat at the hands of Danny McShain. The match ended after 53 seconds when Mitchell suffered a neck injury thanks to a pile driver from McShain. Seeing such a popular babyface go down in such a quick and violent manner made McShain a must-see heel and the new face fans wanted to slap at the wrestling shows.

For many years the story circulated that Danny McShain killed two men with his pile driver finish: Terry McGinnis and Alex Kasaboskie. McShain's nephew Danny Daymon has managed to debunk both of those claims.

The Oregon papers reported that Mitchell would need some time off to heal from the injury. Mitchell traveled back to Ohio, where he nursed himself back to health by getting right back in the ring. Mitchell no-showed his first advertised appearance in Akron due to an illness, but he was soon back in the ring in Fremont, Akron, Marion, Mansfield, and all the old familiar places.

Like many wrestlers of his generation, Mitchell had an eye to the future and a good mind for business. He knew that wrestling would not last forever, and while he was just a decade into his wrestling career, he was already working on what was next. During this particular Ohio run, Mitchell was already promoting his first outside venture, a barbecue restaurant in Toledo, Ohio. The venture had earned him a new nickname at the wrestling shows, "The Spare Ribs King of Toledo," and sports writers suggested that he was giving his sales pitch in the ring to his opponents, even while wearing them down into submission.

Mitchell worked a much lighter schedule in Ohio, suggesting he really was slowing down a bit to develop his new business in Toledo. He stuck mainly to the North Central Ohio region, working towns like Fremont, Sandusky, and Mansfield, that were within 120 miles of home and the restaurant.

In late 1940 and early 1941 Mitchell found himself working with journeyman Antone "Ripper" Leone. Leone was a solid mid-card heel in his time, a perfect opponent for Mitchell, who later worked as a manager. He was best known for his very open hatred for the National Wrestling Alliance. Many men spoke out against the NWA when their monopolistic tactics came to light, but Leone was an especially vocal critic of the group. On his Legacy of Wrestling website, historian Tim Hornbaker writes, "In all of my years of research, I've never seen evidence of any single individual documenting their hatred for the National Wrestling Alliance like Leone did."

Mitchell made a long-awaited return to Fremont, Ohio on April 4, wrestling against Angelo Savoldi. The *News-Messenger* article in Fremont also listed the prices for seats: 44 cents and 65 cents including tax. Kids' seats were only a dime. Translated into 2018 money, the tickets were roughly eight to twelve dollars for adults and $1.75 for kids.

The Black Panther made some return visits to another familiar territory north of the state line in Michigan. Mitchell crossed paths with one of the era's biggest attractions up in Battle Creek, "The French Angel" Maurice Tillet. Born in Russia in 1903 to French parents, Tillet was not a traditional big man, standing only 5'9" but Tillet, who suffered from acromegaly, had an enlarged head, hands, and other features that gave him a monstrous appearance. His physical features made him a natural heel in the ring, but he was known as a kind-hearted and gentle man in real life. Tillet served his native France for five years as an engineer, and there are rumors, yet to be confirmed, he might have worked as a spy, possibly in the same spy ring with the legendary Josephine Baker. Rumor also has it Tillet was the physical inspiration for the title character in the animated classic Shrek. Side by side images of Tillet and Shrek make this rumor and easy one to believe.

In August Mitchell traveled back to Louisville for an engagement against Seelie Samara. Samara was billed as Haille Samara by promoter Heywood Allen, and he had recently dethroned Jack Claybourne as the Negro World Heavyweight Championship. Samara defeated Mitchell to retain his world title at the outdoor Sports Arena Allen had built at the corner of Preston and Burnet Streets in Louisville. In September Mitchell traveled with Samara to Missouri, where he was known as "Ras Samara," for a series of matches in which the same Negro World Title was on the line.

Mitchell made the rounds in the territory with fellow African American Rufus Jones. Jones took on the role of the more heel-like persona in their battles while Mitchell did his usual best to keep it clean. A well-established veteran, Mitchell was already trying to pay it forward to the next generation of stars by helping Jones gain some traction with fans. Little did he know his brightest days were still ahead.

Of course, some truly dark days would come first, not just for Mitchell but the United States and the world. On December 7, 1941, the United States was drawn into the conflict known as World War II. Like most of his contemporaries, Jim Mitchell knew it was only a matter of time before he would be called upon to serve his country.

A gentle and kind spirit in real life, the French Angel Maurice Tillet turned a physical deformity into a main event gimmick. It's hard to argue with the theory that he was the true inspiration for *Shrek*.

The Allen Club
Proudly Presents

TUESDAY

At Sports Arena
Preston and Burnett

Another Colossal
WRESTLING
Program of Unusual Bouts

**NEGRO CHAMPION
HAILLE SAMARA**

Vs.

**LOUISVILLE'S OWN
'BLACK PANTHER'**

390-LB. HIPPO WIGGINS
Vs.
SR. IGNACIO MARTINEZ
All 300-Pounders Free!

Roy
Welch Vs. Red
Roberts

SOLDIERS' SPECIAL
Any Man In Uniform
Admitted for 15c, State
and Federal Taxes

Tickets On Sale
45c, 55c, 75c, $1.00
Seelbach No. 328—JA 1131

Jim Mitchell faced Haille (Seelie) Samara in his return to Louisville
August 26, 1941.

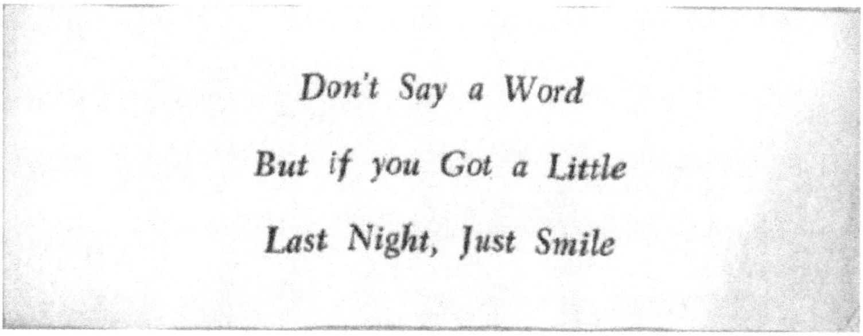

Don't Say a Word

But if you Got a Little

Last Night, Just Smile

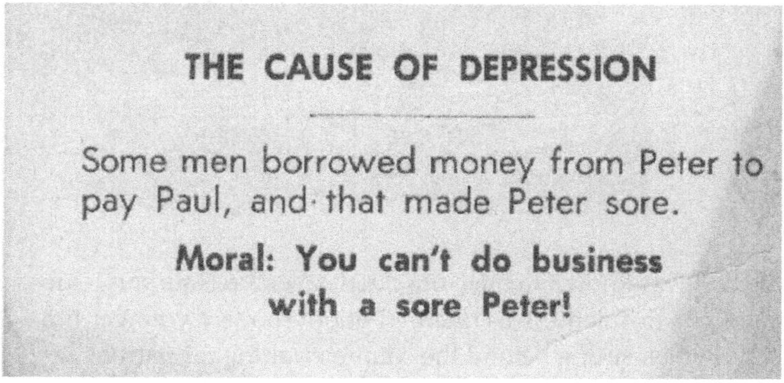

THE CAUSE OF DEPRESSION

Some men borrowed money from Peter to pay Paul, and that made Peter sore.

Moral: You can't do business with a sore Peter!

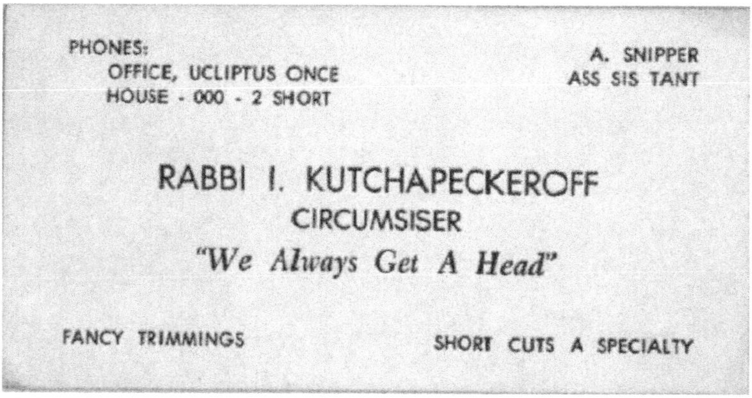

PHONES:
OFFICE, UCLIPTUS ONCE
HOUSE - 000 - 2 SHORT

A. SNIPPER
ASS SIS TANT

RABBI I. KUTCHAPECKEROFF
CIRCUMSISER
"We Always Get A Head"

FANCY TRIMMINGS

SHORT CUTS A SPECIALTY

A collection of cards found among Mitchell's possessions - joke cards the boys passed around in the locker room.

Mitchell was known to have operated several restaurants, clubs, and bars in Toledo. This undated photo shows a younger Jim Mitchell sitting behind the counter waiting for patrons.

SGT. JAMES MITCHELL, US ARMY (1942-1946)

When President Franklin Delano Roosevelt asked for a declaration of war following the attack on Pearl Harbor, it was only a matter of time before America would be calling on all fit, able-bodied men to serve in the conflict. The war would revitalize many industries and bring the United States economy fully out of the Great Depression, but a good number of businesses would suffer while the "boys" were away.

Professional wrestling fell squarely into the latter category. From 1942 through 1945, promoters who had already been struggling to keep their shows afloat found it difficult to find enough men to put on their weekly wrestling shows. It became a boom time for female wrestlers, led by the great champion Mildred Burke, as well as "freaks" who were unfit for military service like the 400-plus pound Hippo Wiggins and the 600-plus pounder "The Blimp."

One change fans saw in the first year of the war was an increase in the number of "Sailors" and "Soldiers" in wrestling. Slapping the moniker "Soldier" or "Sailor" in front of your name was bound to make one an instant babyface for those who supported the cause, and everyone from "Sailor" Fred Blassie to "Sailor" Tug Carlson took full advantage. Mitchell found himself working against Sailor Nelson, Sailor Barto Hill, and other military men as the war effort began.

The cornerstone of the business during the war was "Wild Bill" Longson of St. Louis. The seasoned veteran had a medical deferment and became the go-to world champion during the war years. Longson was a big draw as a heel, and he moved enough tickets to keep the business alive while his contemporaries fought the Axis overseas.

Mitchell would be one of the many wrestlers who would apply his talents to the Armed Forces, but he would not be summoned right away. Mitchell was still slinging spare ribs and wrestling the occasional show in Northern Ohio and Michigan as 1942 began.

Mitchell found himself in an unlikely tag team in early 1942, partnering with Rufus Jones against Billy Rayburn and Steve Nenoff. What made the combination so unusual was that Rayburn, Nenoff, and Mitchell were all regarded as babyfaces while Jones had played the heel in previous bouts against Mitchell. Much ado was made about the fact that Mitchell refused to stoop to Jones's level and insisted on a clean match against the highly successful team of Rayburn and Nenoff. Jones got in some of his signature dirty play, but by and large, the match was by the book. The African American duo handed Rayburn and Nenoff their first loss as a team, but not without some bickering on Jones's part that Mitchell would not bend a few rules when Jones got in trouble.

By summer time, Mitchell knew he was bound for service. *The Marion Star* made mention of this in June, when Mitchell was a no-show for a scheduled wrestling event in that town on June 11. The following day Mitchell took two-out-of-three falls from Sailor Olsen in Fremont.

Mitchell feuded with Rufus Jones some more that summer, usually getting the best of Jones in the process. Former rival turned promoter Les Fisbaugh laid claim that Mitchell was becoming a little rougher when necessary, once again departing from his image as a clean fighter.

By August, the territory was down to one African American star, that being Rufus Jones. At age 34 Jim Mitchell became a member of the United States Army, and after completing basic training, he was assigned to the 10th Air Squadron, an all-black division based in Florence, South Carolina.

The 10th Aviation Squadron was activated on March 24, 1942 at Dale Mary Field in Florida but transferred to South Carolina two months later on May 24th. Squadron commander Captain Earl E. Frink was a beloved leader who strove to give his men all the comforts allowed within the confines of army life. The 10th had its own barbershop, pressing machine, and tailoring ship. They had a glee club that performed weekly on the radio. They also had their own pool room and a day room with new, comfortable furniture that made for a home-like atmosphere.

The 10th also had a mascot, a long-haired white goat who earned his title when he began responding to the call of "Reveille" to watch the men line up in formation. The men of the 10th named him Yardbird.

Mitchell was a physical education instructor for the 10th Aviation Squadron, an ideal role for a man who had always taken health and physical fitness so seriously. Like many wrestlers, Mitchell was a trained shooter, and he passed on much of his knowledge to his fellow soldiers by teaching them hand to hand combat.

Mitchell also took on the role of athletic director for the 10th Aviation Squadron. Mitchell's mementos from the era confirm that he was the athletic director. Mitchell organized a basketball team and solicited games from nearby military divisions and colleges. Mitchell kept copies of letters mailed to other army bases and nearby schools soliciting games for the basketball team. The letters were all signed, "Cpl. James Mitchell, Athletic Director, 10th Air Squadron (SEP)."

Incidentally, a second masked Black Panther, known by the very clever nickname "Black Panther II," began working in California while Mitchell was wrapping up his service. Black Panther II was hoping to capitalize on the success of his predecessor Wee Willie Davis a few years prior, but his run ended not with an unmasking, but an injury. He suffered defeat and a broken leg at the hands of Dutch Hefner on March 3 in Los Angeles.

Mitchell resumed his wrestling career in 1944 after he was honorably discharged from the Army, serving eighteen months. Based out of Toledo, Sgt. Jimmy Mitchell was a bigger, stronger athlete than the Black Panther of 1930, tipping the scales at a solid 240 pounds. He started wrestling on shows in Toledo, Akron, Detroit, and Adrian, Michigan, feuding with old friend Rufus Jones and fellow Kentuckian Irish McGee. He also crossed over into Indiana to work in Muncie, where he crossed paths with Billy Thom, the legendary Indiana University wrestling coach who led the 1936 Olympic team and helped launch the career of Hoosier grappler Dory Funk, Sr.

Many fans saw the return of the popular Black Panther as a sign that wrestling might be making a comeback. Although the D-Day invasion was still a few months away and the war far from over, seeing an old favorite return to the ring better than ever was a sign of hope. Fans were eager for the war to be over, and everyone wanted to see their friends, neighbors, and favorite wrestlers return home so that life could get back to normal.

Two major life moments occurred during the spring of 1944. On April 6 he was granted a certificate of divorce from his first wife, listed in the document only as Ruth L. Mitchell. Ten days later, Mitchell married a woman named Julia Harter of Toledo. Julia was nearly a decade Mitchell's senior, born in 1900. She had been married twice before to Robert L. Blaine, whose occupation was a chauffeur, and Albertus B. Conn, a lawyer who served as the assistant attorney general for the state of Ohio and was a key leader in the state's Republican Party. Julia had a daughter from her marriage to Robert Blaine named Roberta, born April 21, 1920, who had been adopted by her second husband Albertus.

A letter handwritten by Mitchell shortly after the marriage became official was sent to the Veteran's Administration requesting that Julia be named as beneficiary of Mitchell's insurance policy.

No doubt there's a great story behind the quick end of Mitchell's first marriage and the speedy rush into marriage number two, a union that lasted until Mitchell's death. Sadly, it appears the juicy details of love and marriage were never written down and have been lost to history.

As summer approached, promoters started offering tag team wrestling, and the fans were eating it up. Mitchell teamed with a number of partners, including future Indianapolis promoter Balk Estes, but most often with his rival Rufus Jones.

Mitchell took a break between May and October, resuming action on October 23 in Detroit. He went back to working his Ohio-Indiana-Michigan circuit with men like Dutch Schultz, Rufus Jones, and Gil LaCrosse. Business was still tough, but some of the old towns were beginning to run shows again. Les Fisbaugh reopened

Fremont, Ohio, in April with a main event featuring Jim Mitchell and Herb Parks of Canada. Eager to help the war effort, Fisbaugh promoted the show as a benefit for Company B's mess fund. Wrestling shows in Fremont were held at the Armory that Company B called home.

When Mitchell left the Army and returned to the ring, he started a ledger book, recording all of his pay offs and expenses. It's very likely Mitchell had always done this, but only two ledgers survived the long decades in his home: one covering 1944 to 1949, and one covering 1955.

The first ledger shows that Mitchell's territory in the mid-1940s included parts of Michigan, Indiana, and Ontario, Canada as well as Northern Ohio. It took only three months before he was working a full schedule, wrestling twenty-five nights out of thirty-one in March. The highest paying cites in the circuit at that time were Hamilton, Ontario ($67), Toledo, Ohio ($50), Flint, Michigan ($50), and Hammond, Indiana ($40). Jackson, Ohio was the low end at $8. Translated into today's dollars, Mitchell made a scant $113 in Jackson and almost $950 for one night in Ontario!

Mitchell's total income for 1944 came to $2143.32, which equates to $30,366.66 today. It's a modest income by today's standards, but again, Mitchell wrestled less than seven months out of the year.

In the spring of 1945 Mitchell renewed an old rivalry with Lon Chaney, who was downright dirty in an April 20 match in Fremont. What started as a true wrestling match devolved into a slug fest, with both men throwing more punches than wrestling holds. A series of punches to the kidney were Mitchell's doom, and Chaney took the win to a chorus of boos.

By this time there were real signs that the wrestling business was on an upswing. In Akron, promoter Walter Moore was forced to turn away fans as a standing-room only crowd enjoyed a 15 minute bout in which Nick Billen defeated the Black Panther. Moore voiced his support for a proposed 7000-seat venue, saying that a larger space was needed to meet the demand of wrestling-hungry fans. With the Allies accepting Germany's unconditional surrender on May 7, it was only a matter of time before the men of the U.S. Armed Forces returned home. A boom was on the horizon, and everyone could sense it was coming.

Mitchell made his return to Piqua, Ohio in May, and in June he returned to the city where he wrestled his first main event, Kokomo, Indiana. In a match that certainly turns the narrative about a "color barrier" on its head, Mitchell faced Rufus Jones in a much ballyhooed "first ever" battle between two African American grapplers in Kokomo. The Black Panther and Rufus Jones delivered an all-out war. According to *The Kokomo Tribune*, the two "did everything to each other except pull up the ring posts and shame each other over the head with them."

Jones, playing the heel, lost the first fall by disqualification due to rough tactics, and shortly thereafter, he was disqualified in the second fall. Jones took a cheap shot at Mitchell as he left the ring, kicking the Black Panther in the back. Mitchell turned around, dove back into the ring, and battered Jones mercilessly until he scored a final three count.

Incidentally, Mitchell recorded some other unique deductible expenses in April of 1944:

Tights - $9.00

Shoes - $10.00

Socks - $5.00

Rubbing Alcohol and Cocoa Butter - $3.50

Baths and Rub Downs - $12.00

Wrestling Bag - $40.00

These unique deductions added up to $79.50, or $1,101 in 2018 dollars.

Mitchell also spent $96 on transportation, $28 on lodging, and $34 on meals during this stretch. He grossed $323.47 for the month, so his net profit for April was $85.97, or $1190 in 2018 dollars.

Mitchell worked a much lighter travel schedule in 1945, traveling only 58 days that year. He records in his ledger a list of medical expenses due to an accident totaling just over $201, though there are no notes as to what the nature of the accident was nor his injuries. His total gross income for the year came to $2016, just a little under his 1944 income.

In early 1946 Mitchell took a handful of dates in Ohio and Indiana, making his final appearance in towns like Lima, Marion, Fort Wayne, and South Bend. From February through July, Mitchell remained in the Midwest but stuck mostly to the Michigan territory. He dipped down to Chicago for a date or two in early summer, but he was no longer working the Northern Ohio region.

Mitchell wrestled against Bert Ruby and then with Bert Ruby as tag partners in Detroit. He faced "Bull" Montana and the Masked Marvel in the Motor City as well. In May Mitchell and Ruby took on the team of Black Jack Mike Kolonis and the notorious Wild Bull Curry.

Mitchell also traveled to Canada during the first half of 1946, spending a total of 28 nights north of the border between January and July. Most shows were in Ontario, and Mitchell kept a separate ledger page for his Canada dates. All and all he grossed $709 on those 28 dates. Transportation costs varied, depending on his destination, from $4 to $13. Lodging remained steady at $3.50 per night and meals typically cost $3 a day.

In July Mitchell left the Midwest behind and headed to Boston, where he would go to work for Paul Bowser. The move meant a prohibitive leap in expenses, since he was no longer able to drive home after shows, but it also meant a significant increase in pay. In June Mitchell grossed $301 in his last full month in Michigan, netting $101 after expenses. In August, his first full month in New England, Mitchell made $784 gross and $327.75 after expenses. On the low end he made $18 a night in some towns, but in Holyoke, Massachusetts on August 28 he made $109. That would be a $1476 pay day in 2018 money.

Mitchell secured lodging at $17.50 per week for the duration of his stay, and on most nights he was able to make it back to his temporary residence rather than racking up additional hotel stays. Meals typically cost $4.25 per day.

Boston was the center of the territory with a weekly show on Thursday nights. Other cities in the territory would run every two to three weeks and included Massachusetts towns Lawrence, Worcester, Holyoke, Salem, and Lynn as well as Hartford, Connecticut; Providence, Rhode Island; and Portland, Maine.

The crowds were much larger in the New England, and Mitchell worked the opening matches most nights after his arrival. He was new in the territory, and the names on the cards were much bigger than most of the shows he had worked in Ohio. A September 19th show headlined by the French Angel drew 4000 people in Boston. Mitchell worked a 20 minute draw with Ted Germaine in the opener. Other opponents during his first four months in New England included the Great Mephisto, Burt Healion, Tiger Tasker, Roland Meeker, and Jack Claybourne.

Mitchell's popularity grew rapidly in the Boston territory, so much so that if his name was in the marquee, you were likely to see a "Standing Room Only" sign at the box office. Asked to explain his appeal, Mitchell said humbly, "I always give my best, and though the other fellow may break the rules and rough me up a bit, I never resort to dirty tactics to gain a decision."

Mitchell was billed as a native of Detroit during his Boston run. He established himself with a number of time limit draws in the opener and the mid-card. He wasn't winning, but winning is hardly the only way to get a new wrestler over in a territory. Mitchell's athleticism and his ability to go the distance showed the fans he belonged and set him up to become a key player in the territory.

More important for Mitchell, his income took a huge leap from 1945. At the end of the year, he grossed $6154.54, or more than $83,000 in 2018 dollars. His expenses were higher due to living on the road, but the net take home was also significantly higher than his earnings back home.

Mitchell also purchased a rental property in April of 1946. He was no longer in the BBQ business, but it's clear Mitchell's plans for a future beyond wrestling had not been derailed by the war. Mitchell was doing extremely well for himself and his new bride. The future was looking bright, and his star was just beginning to rise.

Sgt. Jim Mitchell and his ever-present pipe with other members of
the 10th Aviation Squadron.

February 11, 1943

Athletic Director (Colored Troops)
Fort Jackson, S. C.

Dear Sir:

Am writing in regards to arranging a basketball game with your team at the earliest date possible. Would like to arrange the game at Fort Jackson. May I hear from you at your earliest convenience?

Yours truly

Cpl. James Mitchell,
Athletic Director,
10th Avn. Sqdn. (Sep)

Mitchell saved copies of a number of letters soliciting basketball games for the 10th Aviation Squadron's hoops team. Letters were also sent to Claflin College, Benedict College, Timmonsville High School, and other military units and schools in South Carolina.

Shooting billiards in uniform. The 10th Aviation Squadron enjoyed their own pool room, one of the many creature comforts provided by their beloved captain.

Mitchell pauses in the middle of a lesson with one of his fellow soldiers, no doubt a welcome break for the unfortunate volunteer upon which Mitchell was demonstrating shoot holds that day.

N.C.O. CLUB
Certificate of Membership

This Certifies That _James "B.A.P" Mitchell_
is a member of the FLORENCE ARMY AIR FIELD
N.C.O. CLUB, (SEP.), FLORENCE, S. C. Said member
is entitled to all rights and privileges of the Club as set
forth in the Constitution and/or By-Laws.

_____ _S/Sgt Clifton Barnett_
Signed   Vice President

Above: Mitchell's NCO Membership card. Below: Mitchell (left
front row) posing with his basketball team.

101

Yardbird, the unofficial mascot of the 10th Aviation Squadron. Yardbird loved to watch the men assemble in formation every morning.

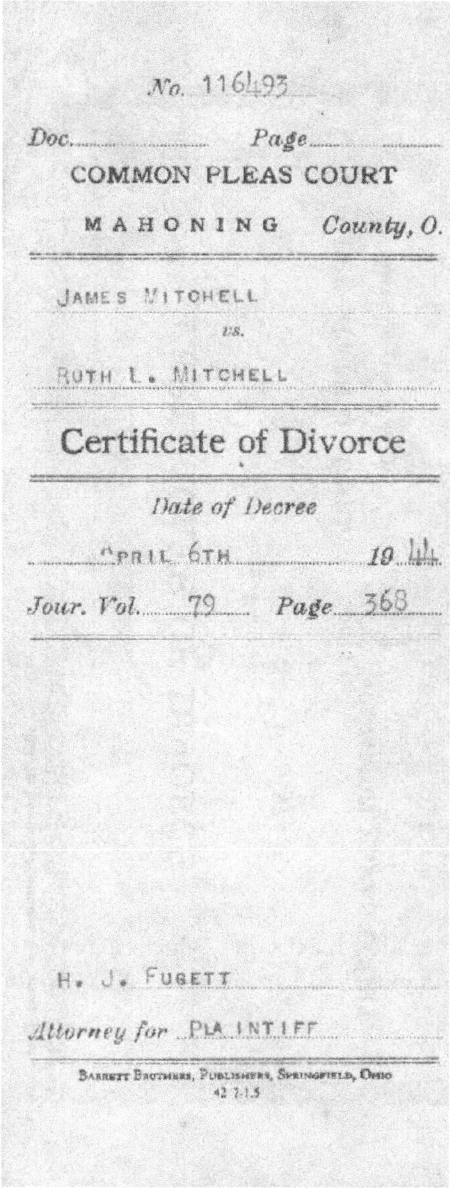

No. 116493

Doc. _____ Page _____

COMMON PLEAS COURT

MAHONING County, O.

JAMES MITCHELL

vs.

RUTH L. MITCHELL

Certificate of Divorce

Date of Decree

APRIL 6TH _____ 19 44

Jour. Vol. 79 *Page* 368

H. J. FUGETT

Attorney for PLAINTIFF

BARRETT BROTHERS, PUBLISHERS, SPRINGFIELD, OHIO
42 7-1.5

Mitchell's first marriage ended April 6, 1944.

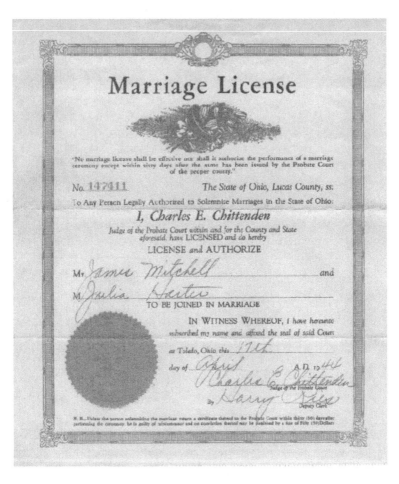

Eleven days later after his divorce, Mitchell married Julia Harter. If these documents could speak, what story would they tell?

Although not labeled, it's my conclusion the photo above is Julia Mitchell, Jim's second wife. Julia was married twice before and had a daughter, Roberta, from her first marriage who was adopted by her second husband, Ohio Republican Albertus B. Conn.

A publicity photo of Mitchell in his prime.

WELCOME TO CALIFORNIA (1947-1948)

In early 1947 Mitchell was pushed into a major storyline already advancing through the Boston territory when he was paired with a masked heel known as Hooded Terror. The Terror had been on an undefeated streak until recently, when he lost a match to Frank Sexton in a disputed finish. The Hooded Terror blamed referee Steve Passas for his loss and was demanding a different referee for his main event confrontation with the Black Panther.

Mitchell lost the battle in a slug fest but proved once again that he belonged in the main event, winning new fans even in defeat. He scored a major victory in the wallet, taking home $160 for the main event spot. That translates to over $1800 in 2018 money.

On January 20 Mitchell appeared on the inaugural card in the town of Fitchburg, Massachusetts. Mitchell faced former Bates College football star Jim Spencer in the opening match. *The Fitchburg Sentinel* proclaimed Mitchell to be the "colored wrestling champion of the world."

Mitchell spent the first nine months traveling the Boston circuit in 1947, taking some time off in March to return home for a break. He wrapped up his New England stint in Boston in September, where his final match - a loss to Reb Russell in the semi-main event - was largely overshadowed by a marquee bout between Tuffy Truesdale and a seven-foot alligator named Rodney.

Mitchell went straight from the East Coast to the West in October, ready to make a statement in the booming Southern California wrestling scene. In the *PAN* wrestling program, Hardy Kruskamp gave Mitchell a tremendous write up upon his arrival. "Called the 'Joe Louis of Matdom' the ex-Black Panther is a former six-day bike rider and also has an impressive boxing record. The Negro champ can handle the roughest and toughest men in the game. He's a rubbery-legged type of grappler, elusive and fast in applying holds. If an opponent would rather square off with his fists, it's all right with the matdom 'Joe Louis,' who can apply a kayo wallop with either elbow or mitt.

"Mitchell started his mat career when a youngster in Detroit, and was so adept that he was contracted for a tour of Europe... Mitchell's speed, aggressiveness and sportsmanship are bound to give local fans plenty of thrills. And his shoulder butts, hip headlocks or drop kicks are due to cause plenty of havoc in the local ranks."

His debut match in Los Angeles was at the Olympic Auditorium, where he faced Carlos Mojica. It was a star-studded evening capped off by a main event featuring California champion Reginald Siki and Mexican star Vincent Lopez. British wrestler Earl McCready wrestled Vic Christy, and Sammy Menacker and Canadian Larry Moquin teamed up to wrestle Killer Karl Davis and Wee Willie Davis, aka the former masked Black Panther of California. As if that wasn't enough star power, the legendary Ed "Strangler" Lewis was promised to be on hand to referee.

Mitchell's $60 payday for his first opening match in the LA Coliseum was far above his average take in Boston. It was another major step up into a territory that, at the time, boasted the biggest names in the business. It would not take Mitchell long to prove he belonged in their company.

The schedule in California was much simpler and less spread out than Boston. Monday was Pasadena. Tuesday, Southgate. Wednesday was at the Olympic Auditorium in LA. Thursday was in Long Beach, and Friday was at Ocean Park. Saturdays and Sundays were off.

Welcome to California.

Mitchell's travel expenses from Boston to Los Angeles cost $175 plus $18 for his luggage. In his first month on the West Coast he also spent $12 at the gym, $20 for massages, $90 for photos, and $25 for "publicity." His meal expenses jumped from $4.25 per day to $5.25 per day, but his monthly lodging fee was cut in half from $70 a month in Boston to $35 in Los Angeles. His monthly gross also saw an immediate boost from $628 in Boston in September to $880 in California in October.

On October 29 the Original Black Panther met the masked Black Panther and his tag partner in a main event at the Olympic. Jim Mitchell teamed up with Manuel Garza to wrestle Karl and Wee Willie Davis in the main event. The Davis boys took the first pin, and Garza and Mitchell the second. The match ended in a draw, with neither team scoring the winning pin before time expired. The show drew 8500 fans, and Mitchell made a whopping $215 that night.

A week later, a two hour time limit was set for the rematch. This time Mitchell and Garza came out on top, defeating the Davis boys. The box office was the same with 8500 in attendance, but Mitchell took home only $160 that night. It was still far larger than anything he had made previously in the Midwest or New England.

On November 12 Mitchell was part of a tournament at the Olympic featuring an international roster of wrestlers. Entrants included Larry Moquin, Ray Duran, Manuel Garza, Mickey Page, Senator Hartford, Vic Christy, Chief War Cloud, Marvin Jones, Kolo Stasiak, Bomber Kulkovich, and Alex Kasaboski. Mitchell had a very strong showing, defeating Senator Hartford in the first round and Ray Duran in the second before losing to Marvin Jones in the semi-final. Larry Moquin of Canada defeated Jones to win the tournament.

In November Mitchell made his debut in a few new locations including Wilmington, Pico, Jeffries Barn, and San Bernardino. Mitchell faced Manuel Garza in the semi-main event in Wilmington on November 18. The main event that night pitted Vic Christy against the former George Wagner of Texas, who had only recently adopted his new ring persona, Gorgeous George.

Mitchell's San Bernardino debut took place on November 21 against Sammy Menacker. The two men battled to a one hour draw, with each wrestler taking one fall a piece. Menacker was hyped as an Army veteran and a well-respected grappler. Once again, the draw proved to be a great way to get Mitchell over with the fans without either man taking a loss.

On November 26 Mitchell appeared in another main event bout at the Olympic. His opponent was Frank Sexton and the prize was Sexton's World Heavyweight Championship. The match was scheduled for two-out-of-three falls with a one hour time limit. Mitchell lost the match before a crowd of 9000 when Sexton put him in a backbreaker, but he took home a payday of $275 that no doubt eased his ailing back.

Just a few days later, Mitchell only made $41 for a tag team main event in which he teamed with Manuel Garza against Jules Strongbow and Gorgeous George. The *Wilmington Daily Press Journal* rightly pointed out that this would actually be a three-on-two match with George's valet Jeffrey at ringside. Referee Ted Grace had his hands full and nearly awarded a win to Mitchell and Garza due to the illegal tactics of George and Strongbow. In the end the villains did just enough to secure a victory over the team of Garza and Mitchell.

The disputed ending was enough to earn the babyfaces a chance at redemption, and redeem themselves they did. A week later it was Mitchell and Garza who came out on top over Gorgeous George and Jules Strongbow.

Mitchell also got a crack at former champion Enrique Torres in San Bernardino on December 13. Mitchell earned a modest $38 in defeat, losing two out of three falls to Torres in a crowd pleaser.

Mitchell was a solid fan favorite heading into 1948, and he was making more money than ever. His total wrestling income for 1947 was $6974 with an additional $383 from his rental properties in Toledo. He was in the right place at the right time, and his biggest year in wrestling was just ahead.

The entire California wrestling scene was on an upswing as 1948 began, due in large part to the rise of Gorgeous George. Although George admittedly borrowed most of his act from Wilbur Finran's Lord Lansdowne, George Wagner took the idea to an extreme Finran never dreamed of. George bleached his hair blonde and had it styled by Hollywood hair stylists Frank and Joseph into a signature 'do known as the "marcel." He wore gold plated bobby pins which he called "Georgie pins" in his hair and presented them to his most loyal female fans. He wore flowing robes of silk and lavender, some reportedly costing upwards of ten thousand dollars.

Men hated him. Women adored him. Promoters loved him.

He was guaranteed money.

Mitchell and other benefitted from being on the cards with George, even if they weren't in the same match. If Gorgeous George's name was on the marquee, you were getting paid well because the fans would show up. Mitchell was working in support matches in early 1948, usually battling foes like Kola Staskiak, Angelo Cistoldi, and Hardy Kruskamp or teaming with Manuel Garza in a tag team, but most nights Gorgeous George was the headliner.

On February 26 Mitchell had what appears to be his first head-to-head confrontation with the Gorgeous One. Promoter Harry Rubin in Long Beach was the matchmaker who booked the two on his usual Thursday night program at the Municipal Auditorium. Sadly, the *Long Beach Independent* did not report the results in the Friday paper, though it's likely the match ended with either a disqualification win for Mitchell or more likely an ill-gotten win for George.

Mitchell had his hands full every night. One minute he was going head to head with 6'4", 300 pound Jules Strongbow, the next he was tangled up with Angelo Savoldi, and the next he was in a tag battle against the likes of the Zaharias brothers, Babe and Chris. The top stars in the country were flocking to California, including Mitchell's old rival Martino Angelo, and business was red hot.

Mitchell's next publicized encounter with Gorgeous George was in Los Angeles at a charity event held at the Hollywood Legion Stadium. The program was a benefit for the Crippled Children's Fund, and promoter Hugh Nichols promised the proceeds from the show would go to the Fund. Also on the card that night were singles matches between Wild Red Berry and Jan Blears, Martino Angelo and Leo Wallick, Sockeye McDonald and Bomber Kulkovich, and Honest John Cretoria and Whitey Whitler. Mitchell took the first fall that night, but George came from behind to score two straight pinfalls and defeat Mitchell. *The Los Angeles Times* did not recap the box office or attendance for the benefit.

In May Jim Mitchell faced Frank Brother Jares, aka the "Mormon Mangler," in San Bernardino. Jares was best known as "The Thing," and his son Joe, a sports writer, penned one of the finest books about the golden era of wrestling ever written, *Whatever Happened to Gorgeous George?* Joe's book was one of several to record Jim Mitchell's most famous bout, a match against Gorgeous George that took place in the summer of 1949, still fifteen months in the future at the time he met up with the Mormon Mangler. Jares and Mitchell battled to a draw, with each man taking one fall in the battle before time expired.

Mitchell worked a short month in May before taking some time off, most likely to head home to Toledo for a spell. He returned to action in July, not in California but back East in the Boston territory. The houses were packed but notably smaller in New England, where Mitchell battled the likes of Canadian Tiger Tasker and Jim Beaton of Lowell, Massachusetts. Before departing, Mitchell put over a red hot masked heel in Boston named Mr. X, who defeated Mitchell in straight falls to continue in his quest to unseat champion Frank Sexton.

Mitchell returned to the West Coast in October, where he resumed a recurring feud with the notorious Zaharias brothers. Mitchell had several partners in his on-going battles against Babe and Chris, but in October he paired with two true heavyweights. On October 6 in Los Angeles, Mitchell received back up in the form of former Chicago Bear and wrestling champion Bronco Nagurski. Nagurski and Mitchell lost that battle, but a week later Mitchell paired with another bruiser in Tug Carlson to face the Zaharias brothers in Long Beach, this time going to a time limit draw.

Mitchell earned his largest payout of the year on November 10 in Los Angeles in a stellar main even matchup against Primo Carnera. A crowd of 9200 people was on hand to watch the former heavyweight boxer take on the very popular Black Panther. Carnera battered Mitchell against the ring posts, causing - at least according to kayfabe - a shoulder injury that forced the referee to give a decision to Carnera. Both men kept their heat as a result of the finish, and Mitchell earned $250 for the night - $2634 by 2018 dollars.

Mitchell teamed with known prankster Vic Christy against Hans and Fritz Schnabel for a tag bout in Wilmington on December 14. The two teams fought to a time limit draw, with both sides claiming one fall. Afterwards, the Schnabels wanted to keep on fighting. Mitchell and Christy were happy to oblige, getting the best of the Schnabels and their manager before chasing them off to the showers.

The "feel good" finale to Mitchell's banner year in California came on December 22 at the Olympic Auditorium. The crowd was light that evening, only 5200 in attendance, when Mitchell took on Bobby Managoff in the main event. Managoff sustained an injury that forced the referee to call the match, but feeling the Christmas spirit, Mitchell refused to be named the winner. The official decision was a draw, and the fans stood and applauded the very popular Black Panther and his wounded opponent.

Mitchell's gross income in wrestling for 1948 came to $8294.50, with an additional $528 in rental revenue back in Toledo bringing the total to $8822.50. Translated into 2018 dollars, Mitchell made $92,947. As he had from the beginning, Mitchell wisely banked a good chunk of money as an investment in his future. He was 40 years old, still in the prime of his career, but 1949 would be the year he and his biggest fans would never forget.

A bigger, bulkier Black Panther made the trek to California in the late 1940s, where he became one of the top draws of the era. His weight varied between 240 and 260 pounds.

Ringside photo in the Olympic Auditorium.

WEE WILLIE DAVIS giving Jim Mitchell, the Black Panther, a rough time in last week's team match. Mitchell turned the tables and sent Willie to defeat with his cranium cracker hold.

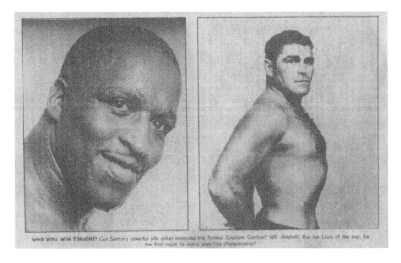

WHO WILL WIN TONIGHT? Can Sexton's powerful elbow driver overcome the famous Cranium Cracker? Will Mitchell, the Joe Louis of the mat, be the first negro to win a wrestling championship?

Promo photos from the Olympic wrestling programs.

Wednesday 22 Dec 1948
11:00 P.M.

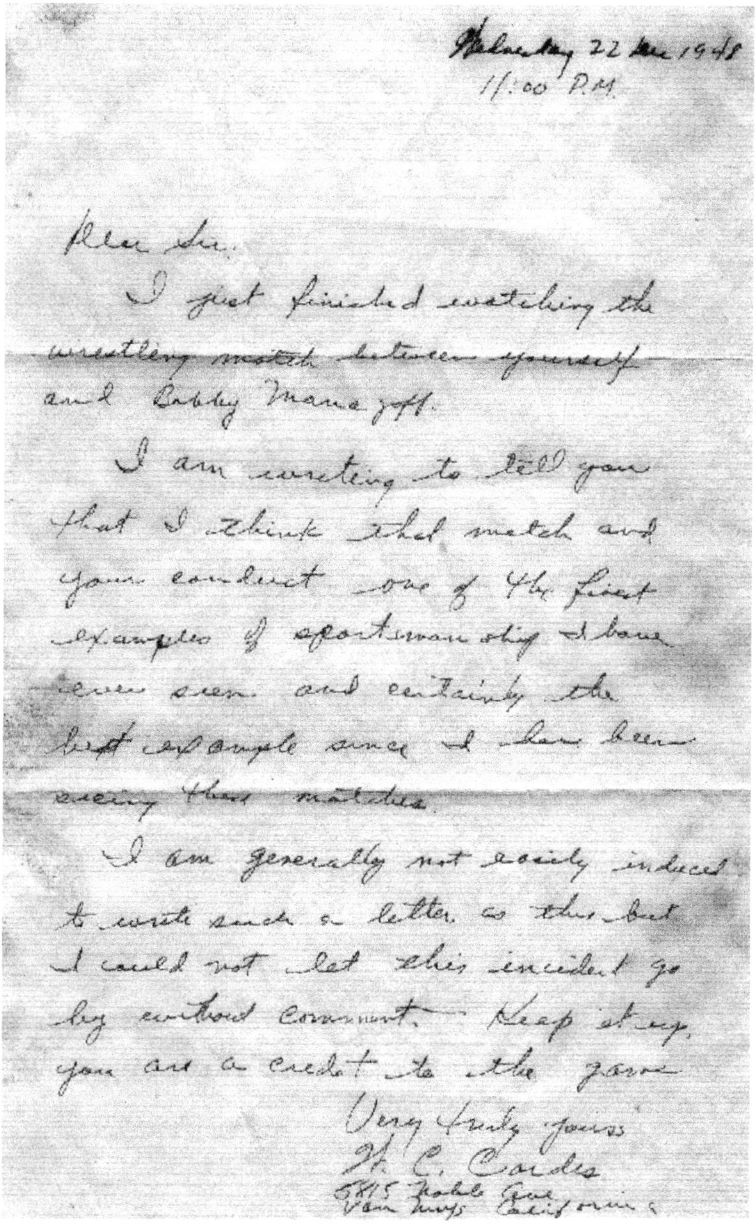

Dear Sir.

I just finished watching the wrestling match between yourself and Bobby Managoff.

I am writing to tell you that I think that match and your conduct one of the finest examples of sportsmanship I have ever seen and certainly the best example since I have been seeing these matches.

I am generally not easily induced to write such a letter as this but I could not let this incident go by without comment. Keep it up, you are a credit to the game

Very truly yours
H. C. Cordes
5815 Noble Ave
Van Nuys California

A fan letter, 1948, praising Mitchell's sportsmanship.

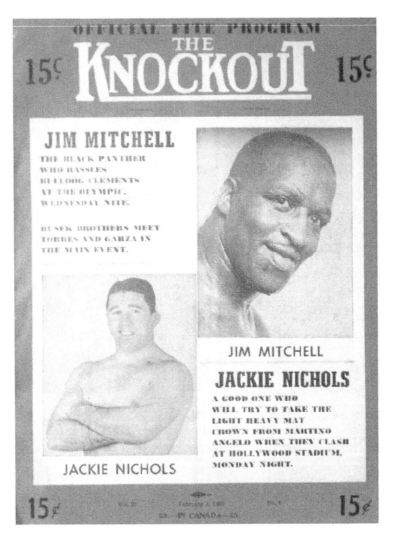

On the cover of the *Knockout* boxing and wrestling program,
February 7, 1948.

The Black Panther heads to the ring, ready for a fight.

Another candid photo of Mitchell in his ring gear.

The Freedom Train was a seven car train that traveled across the country. The traveling museum contained a number of important American documents from the National Archives and the Library of Congress including the Declaration of Independence and the Bill of Rights. The purpose was to let everyone in America have access to view these documents and celebrate America's historical heritage. Cities that hosted the Freedom Train were required to allow blacks and whites to view the documents together, with no segregation. Memphis, Tennessee, and Birmingham, Alabama, refused to let the train stop due to this requirement. The group above includes Mexican wrestler Enrique Torres (fourth from left), Gorgeous George (second from right), and Jim Mitchell near center.

Mr. Box-Office of 1948 Returns to Local Mat Wars

Side by side with Gorgeous George in *PAN*, a year before the most famous match of Jim Mitchell's career with the Human Orchid.

RIOT IN LOS ANGELES (1949)

In early 1949 Mitchell began a heated feud with British nobleman Lord Blears. Known in the press as "England's Gorgeous George," His Lordship was hardly the first man who claimed to be of royal bearing, nor was he the most famous of his time. He was, however, more authentic than the likes of Lord Patrick Lansdowne and Lord Leslie Carlton (aka Tug Carlson) because he was in fact British. Mitchell worked against Blears in several towns in January and February, as a singles and tag opponent with numerous partners on both sides. Both sides would win on different nights, but one victory over Blears was used to put Mitchell in the number one contender spot to face a new top villain in the territory - Wild Bill Longson.

A Hall of Fame legend who, sadly, has largely been overlooked and forgotten by many, Bill Longson was a fixture in Mitchell's hometown of Louisville for nearly two decades. He was also the only man to ever win a major professional wrestling championship in Louisville (a story you can read in *Bluegrass Brawlers* and *Louisville's Greatest Show*), but it wasn't until Longson made his way to California that the native Louisvillian got a shot at the man who was arguably the biggest draw in Louisville's history.

In April Mitchell worked against Gorgeous George in Van Nuys and again in Burbank at the grand re-opening of Jeffries Barn. Located at the corner of Victory Boulevard and Buena Vista Avenue, Jeffries Barn was a boxing and wrestling venue owned and operated by former heavyweight boxer James Jeffries. Jeffries owned 107 acres, including the property where the barn sat, and after several false starts became very successful as a cattle rancher. The barn held 1100 people, and during the weekly boxing matches on Thursday nights, fans rubbed shoulders with celebrities like Cary Grant, Mae West, and Al Jolson. After Jeffries' death in 1953, the barn was disassembled and transported to Knotts Berry Farm, where it was

123

reassembled and used as a boxing museum, a haunted attraction, and a dance hall.

Mitchell left California in mid-April to work two weeks in Texas for Morris Siegel. He spent $97.87 on plane fare, plus $5.20 for baggage, to make the trip, where he twice worked the loop: Fort Worth to Dallas to San Antonio to Galveston to Houston. He appears to have wrestled Don Kindred every night during his Texas trip, working time limit draws or "Broadways" with him every night up until the April 28 show in Galveston when Mitchell finally pinned him.

Mitchell was back in California by May 2. He dropped a few singles main events to Enrique Torres and renewed his tag rivalry against Lord Blears. He paired up with Torres to take on the "Dirty" Duseks at the Olympic in front of 7900 on May 25. On June 14 he went to a time limit draw in Wilmington against George Temple, the brother of movie star Shirley Temple. On June 25 he met Gorgeous George again in Burbank, and in July he had a series of back and forth battles against Vick Holbrook.

July 31, 1949, Jim Mitchell turned 41 years old. It was a Sunday, and Mitchell had the night off as usual. Twenty-four days later, 9700 fans packed into the Olympic Auditorium to see Mitchell square off with a now familiar foe, the Toast of the Coast, Gorgeous George. It was a night that would live in infamy.

The former George Wagner was now firmly entrenched as the biggest wrestling star on the West Coast. He had recently wrapped filming on the movie *Alias the Champ*, and in short time, he would become a household name across the United States. As much as Milton Berle deserves credit for putting televisions in homes all across the country, Gorgeous George sold just as many TVs, if not more.

Mitchell and George had met numerous times by now. They were a perfect pairing. Mitchell was the clean, honest babyface who played by the rules and made the fans proud. George was the scoundrel, the cheat, always looking for a short cut. Every match prior to the August 24 main event had ended with a George victory or a draw, but Mitchell had kept things just close enough to give fans hope that maybe the next time, he would finally give George what was coming to him.

"Ladies and gentlemen," the ring announcer cried, "Gorgeous George is coming!"

George entered in his usual grand manner, accompanied by his attendant Jeffries. Jeffries performed his pre-match duties, including spraying the ring and George's opponent with the perfume atomizer. George always got a laugh when he announced his fragrance was Chanel No. 10 instead if Chanel No. 5, saying, "Why be half safe?" But when Jeffries sprayed Mitchell with the perfume, Mitchell's fans seethed with anger.

It was already a hot summer evening when the main event began, and the tension was high throughout the match. Mitchell played by the rules as a good babyface should, and every time George bent the rules, Mitchell's fans inched closer to the edge of their seats.

The tipping point came as Mitchell attempted a flying tackle on the Human Orchid. George side-stepped the maneuver and delivered a cheap shot to Mitchell, who fell out of the ring. The referee pronounced Mitchell unable to continue the match and named Gorgeous George the winner.

No sooner was the match ended that another fight broke out. An angry fan charged the ring, intent on making Gorgeous George pay for his cowardly actions. George leg-dived the man and swept him off his feet before vacating the ring and crawling into a tunnel beneath the ring that led to the dressing room. The timekeeper Jack Smith blocked the entrance to the tunnel with a chair just as the crowd rose up en masse. The arena split along racial lines and a riot erupted.

A man from Azusa named Claude M. Bullard was stabbed in the right shoulder. A friend of Bullard's named Lee Howard suffered a broken thumb as he tried to help Bullard to safety. A woman named Norma Romero took a blackjack to the eye. The battle raged until nearly 4 a.m. before the cops could restore order, and nearby Georgia Receiving Hospital had an unusually busy evening.

"The fighting spread from the ring into the aisles and seats and even continued outside the building," said *The Los Angeles Times* on August 25. "Police stationed at the auditorium finally restored order, but scores of additional officers were dispatched to stand by while the building was emptied."

Mitchell and George were both injured in the fracas, but neither man suffered any serious damage. They were treated at the arena and released. Mitchell finished out the week wrestling in Long Beach on Thursday, Oceanside Friday, and San Bernardino on Saturday.

On Monday August 29, the California State Athletic Commission sent a letter to Mitchell. Signed by Assistant Secretary Clayton W. Frye, the letter was an order to appear at the offices of the Golden State Mutual Life Insurance Company in Los Angeles at 3:30 p.m. on August 31 "for a Commission hearing concerning violations of wrestling rules in the exhibition in which you participated at the Olympic Auditorium on Wednesday, August 24th, 1949." Mitchell kept the letter, and it was found among his possessions decades later. My guess is Gorgeous George likely received a similar notice.

Four months later, both Mitchell and George were named in a lawsuit filed in the wake of the August riot. Claude Bullard, his wife Esther, and another wounded spectator sued George, Mitchell, matchmaker Babe McCoy, and booking agents Johnny Doyle and Alvah M. Eaton for the then whopping sum of $30,000. In addition to the stab wound, Bullard alleged that Mitchell fell on top of him during the melee. Mrs. Bullard also claimed to have been injured, and Morelock claimed to have suffered a relapse of wartime shell shock.

While the lawsuit generated a great deal of press, the result from the lawsuit has yet to be discovered. It's pure speculation whether Gorgeous George and Jim Mitchell had to pay up for the harm they caused. In 2018 the promoter and the wrestlers would have paid heavily in such a lawsuit, but in 1949, it's far more likely George and Mitchell escaped without losing a dime.

The story of the riot made headlines across California, appearing in most of the towns where Mitchell and George worked. Newspapers as far away as New Jersey also picked up the story.

While Gorgeous George was back in action in California in September, it appears Mitchell took a great deal more heat for the incident. Regardless of who was to blame, if anyone, Gorgeous George was the bigger star, and sending George into exile would have been much more costly than sending Jimmy Mitchell away.

Mitchell dropped $187.93 to fly from California to New York. He recorded additional expenses of $9, $5, and $10 for wrestling licenses in New York, New Jersey, and Pennsylvania. After a few weeks off, he returned to action on September 15 in Ridgewood Grove, Brooklyn, and the publicity from the August 24 riot made him a red hot attraction on the East Coast.

The average payouts in the East were not a significant drop from what Mitchell was used to in LA, but the big pay days he received from major events and the weekly Olympic shows were gone. After making $240 for his history-making fight on August 24 with Gorgeous George, Mitchell's biggest pay day in September was only $35. After working with Lord Jan Blears, Gorgeous George, and Enrique Torres month after month, he found himself working main events in October against "1-Ton Elmer Estep," a mountain of a man from Arkansas whose actual weight was just over 400 pounds.

The New York press played up Mitchell's previous connections to New England, claiming that while he was born in Louisville, he grew up in Massachusetts. It was the first time he was billed primarily as Jim Mitchell and not the Black Panther. This also appears to be the time frame when Mitchell became known for the "cranium cracker," a head butt he used as a finishing move. It's likely that Mitchell transitioned from the shoulder butt/tackle he had previously used to the head butt as a way to reduce the wear and tear on his body after two decades in the ring.

The East Coast press and promoters sold Mitchell as a solid all-around athlete, which he was, and Mitchell quickly got over with the fans. He made a $200 main event payout in Newark on October 28 and earned a few $100 payouts in November, boosting his earnings for those two months to $964 and $765.

In December Mitchell found the man who would become his next great rival: Gene Stanlee. "Mr. America," as he was known, was born Eugene Stanley Zygowicz on New Year's Day, 1917, to Polish immigrants. He was partially paralyzed as a child after falling down a flight of stairs and even given last rites, but after seeing a strongman at his church, he was inspired. He started wrestling and working out, creating his own homemade gym with iron that he carried off from a local rail yard. He became a champion body builder. He joined the Navy during World War II and served in the South Pacific, where he also started wrestling. He earned enough notoriety among his fellow sailors that when the war ended, promoters started calling.

Mitchell earned a respectable $52 for a December 16 match up with Stanlee in Jamaica, New York. He finished the year with $8171 in total wrestling income, plus another $528 from his rental property in Toledo.

JEFFRIES BARN
WRESTLING NEWS

| VOL. 1 | SATURDAY, JUNE 25, 1949 | No. 10 |

TOAST OF THE COAST -- GORGEOUS GEORGE -- RETURNS TO JEFFRIES BARN: BATTLES 'BLACK PANTHER' JIM MITCHELL IN MAIN EVENT!

VIC CHRISTY TACKLES HANS SCHNABEL In Semi-Windup

GORGEOUS (himself)

THE BLACK PANTHER

| DAVE LEVIN TO MEET STRODE | | KENNEDY FACES MORRIE SHAPIRO |

The envy of the fashion world, but the scourge of the mat ranks, Gorgeous George will head Jeffries Barn's sensational wrestling show tonight. Hailed as the "Toast of the Coast" —"The Orchid Man"—or "Mr. Television" by the press, but simply as POISON by other wrestlers, the Gorgeous One will collide with Jim Mitchell in the roaring main event.

The bleached and beautiful George will be attired in one of his most dazzling robes for his Barn entrance, and will be, of course, attended by his valet-body-guard.

Another record crowd will be on hand — not to cheer George, but maddened by the Orchid's vile treatment of Bobby Becker here two weeks' ago, — hope to see him, for once, get a dose of his own bad medicine.

And the man best qualified really to turn the heat on George is the Black Panther. Aside from his dangerous cranium-crackers, choking cravats and slamming shoulder butts, Mitchell also specializes in a hangman's hold.

VALLEY STARS IN SEMI-WINDUP

Vic Christy, streamlined powerhouse, one of the world's greatest flying body-scissors experts, will be up against the Dutch terrorist, Hans Schnabel, in the semi-windup. There long has been bitter rivalry between the Christy and Schnabel families, and now that Vic has returned to his Van Nuys home from Australia and Hans is back at his Chatsworth farm from a Chicago invasion, these famed stars' Barn battle has every making of a hill-billy feud.

Dave Levin, former world-champion, returns here tonight to tangle with that great football star and fast-developing mat man, Woody Strode. And of main event caliber will be the meeting of these powerful, scientific wrestling idols.

The opening classic also would be good for a main event in any arena, as Jack Kennedy, colorful Texas cowperhouse, will collide with matdom's "Little Hercules" Morrie Shapiro.

IT'S ANOTHER BIG NIGHT AT THE BARN:
BE HERE EARLY!

(Doors open at 7 p.m. for bleacher seats)

Program cover for a June 1949 rematch at Jeffries Barn.

129

Program cover from August 24, 1949 - the night of the riot.

JAMES A. ANDERSON, Director
Department of Professional and
Vocational Standards

FRED A. TAYLOR
Assistant Director

Earl Warren
Governor

COMMISSION MEMBERS

ABRAHAM M. CLOWNING
SHERMAN O. HOUGHTON
DAVID K. STEVENSON
MARSH L. FOSTER
JOE E. BROWN

J. W. DONNELLY
SECRETARY

STATE OF CALIFORNIA

State Athletic Commission

611 MONEY LAUGHLIN BUILDING
315 SOUTH BROADWAY
LOS ANGELES 13, CALIFORNIA

August 29, 1949

Mr. James Mitchell
1550 South Eastern Avenue
Los Angeles, California

Dear Sir:

Please consider this letter an order to appear
at the offices of the Golden State Mutual Life Insurance
Company, 1999 West Adams Boulevard, Los Angeles on
Wednesday, August 31st, 1949 at 2:30 P. M. for a Commission
hearing concerning violation of wrestling rules in the
exhibition in which you participated at the Olympic
Auditorium on Wednesday, August 24th, 1949.

Yours truly,

Clayton W. Frye
Assistant Secretary
State Athletic Commission

CWF:mk

Mitchell received the letter above ordering him to appear and answer for his part in the riot that took place on August 24. Shortly after this, he flew east to New York.

august		1949	
aug 1	Pico		20.00
" 3	Olympic		120.00
" 4	Long Beach		25.00
" 5	Ocean Park		30.00
" 6	San Bernardino		20.00
" 8	Pasadena		18.00
" 11	Long Beach		25.00
" 12	Ocean Park		30.00
" 13	San Bernardino		25.00
" 15	Pasadena		18.00
" 16	Southgate		17.00
" 17	Olympic		40.00
" 18	Long Beach		25.00
" 19	Oceanside		35.00
~~" 20~~	~~San Bernardino~~		
" 23	South Gate		20.00
" 24	Olympic		240.00
" 25	Long Beach		25.00
" 26	Oceanside		25.00
" 27	San Bernardino		20.00
			753.00

Mitchell's ledger book for August 1949. Note the $240 payday for
August 24 at the Olympic.

Phone.	Hotel & Rooms @ 5	Meals Per day @ 5.75	Auto Mileage	Wrestling Clothes	Other items
3.00					
3.50				Shoes	7.50
2.50					
7.00			5.00	8.50	
3.00					
3.50					
3.50					
7.00					
3.00					1.75
2.50			5.00		
3.50					
10.00					
					1.50
2.50			5.00		
3.50					
10.00					
7.00					
74.00	155.00	178.25	15.00	8.50	17.75

Telephone L.C. to N.Y. 6.75

V
W
X
Z

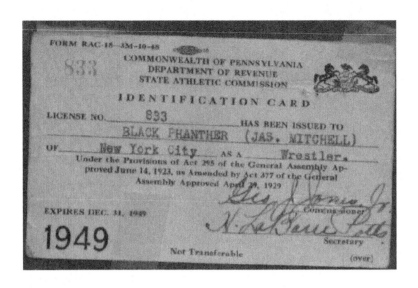

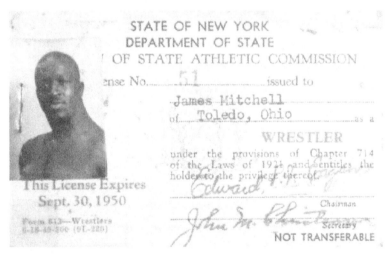

By September, Mitchell was licensed to work in New York, New Jersey, and Pennsylvania. Two of his three new licenses are pictured above.

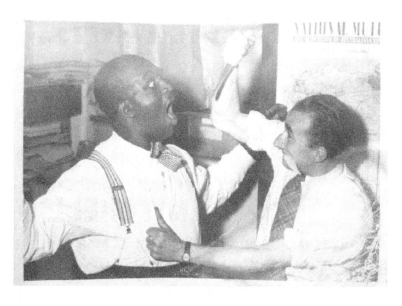

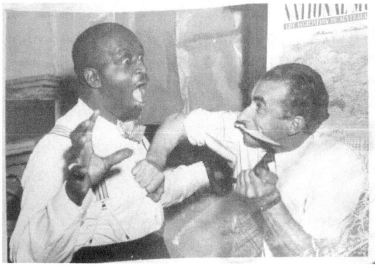

Two hilarious photos Mitchell saved with the notorious Jack Pfefer. I have the top photo. Jim Cornette has the bottom.

Jim Mitchell found a new favorite opponent in New York - Mr. America, Gene Stanlee.

TV OR NOT TV (1950-1951)

Jim Mitchell opened the year 1950 with a January 4 match in Philadelphia against Petro Ortega. Two days later, Mitchell wrestled in New York City against Ivan Kamiroff. If the photo in the newspaper ad is accurate, Kamiroff was actually Tor Johnson, the "Super Swedish Angel," who later starred in the 1950s classic films *Bride of the Monster* and *Plan 9 from Outer Space*. That said, it's very likely the newspaper or promoter put the wrong photo in the ad. This was not uncommon in most places, as evidenced by an ad that appeared in the Carolinas featuring Jim Mitchell's photo long after he retired.

Mitchell's Friday, January 6 appearance in New York may come as a surprise to wrestling fans who were in Greely, Colorado that same night. After a last minute cancellation by Golden Superman, it was announced that the Black Panther Jim Mitchell would be wrestling against Mr. America in Greely, two time zones away. Odds are when Golden Superman canceled, the Colorado promoter grabbed the first replacement he could find, in this case another African American, and slapped a well-known name on him. Mitchell had made headlines far and wide after the LA riot, so the story fits.

The explanation may sound terribly racist, but it's the sort of thing that happened with wrestlers of all races and backgrounds when a cancellation happened, not just African Americans. Case in point, a story I've told in two previous books: a Wisconsin grappler working under the name Bob Fredericks was a no-show for an appearance in Louisville, Kentucky in early January of 1913, so another new wrestler was sent out as "Bob Fredericks." When the real Bob Fredericks showed up a few weeks later, the promoter told him he couldn't go on as Bob Fredericks for fear of tipping the fans that the business wasn't an honest one. A new moniker was bestowed on the original Bob Fredericks, and that night in

Louisville, the world met Ed "Strangler" Lewis for the first time.

All that said, it's very likely that the "Mr. America" who had been scheduled in Greely was not Gene Stanlee, and entirely possible that the "Golden Superman" was not the real Golden Superman either. "Fake Jim Mitchell" worked a number of matches in the Colorado territory that winter, and it's safe to say he had a much better run than either Fake Diesel or Fake Razor Ramon had for Vince McMahon in the 1990s.

Mitchell had plenty to keep him busy on the East Coast. He worked a series of bouts with Miguel Torres in January. On January 20, Mitchell's main event go against Antonino Rocca was broadcast live on WOR radio at 9 p.m.. On Tuesday the 24th of January his main event bout against the real "Mr. America" Gene Stanlee was not only broadcast on WCBS radio but on WCAU television.

In March Jim Mitchell worked a program with the real Golden Superman, who was with him in the New York territory. Golden Superman was Walter Podolak, one of the most famous body builders of his day. His good looks and physique would have made him an attraction enough, but Golden Superman wore a cape to the ring along with head gear that looked like a cross between an amateur boxer's safety gear and something out of the *Flash Gordon* serials.

Mitchell and Golden Superman worked a main event series all over the territory in February. It was a dream matchup for the fans, many of whom had asked to see the two fan favorites step in the ring together. It was to be Mitchell's last run across the East Coast, as Southern California was once again calling. Mitchell put Golden Superman over, and in March, he headed West once more.

Fans were thrilled to see Mitchell return after his six month hiatus, and Mitchell wasted no time getting back in the mix with opponents like Babe Zaharias, Marvin Jones, and a 252-pound ruffian known as the Masked Marvel. San Bernardino fans got an extra treat on April 1 when Mitchell agreed to take on Jim Kolima and Hi Billings in a two-on-one semi-handicap match. The stipulation for this bout was that if Mitchell lost, he would forfeit his payday for the match. The newspaper wasn't kind enough to cover the results the following day, and Mitchell didn't keep the ledger for 1950 that would reveal whether or not he actually got paid. Mitchell was too good of a business man to wrestle for free, so win or lose, it's doubtful he walked away empty-handed.

Mitchell returned to a wrestling scene in transition in California. Television was a hot topic among fans, promoters, and wrestlers, and while the new medium would prove to be a huge boon to wrestling in the long run, the jury was still out in 1950. Television stations were eager to fill their weekly schedules with as much programming as possible, and of all major sports, wrestling was the easiest to broadcast. Wrestling had proven to be very popular with viewers, and the sport is credited with putting televisions into a large number of homes in Southern California and across the country.

After an initial spike in attendance, the weekly box office dropped in most California towns once television came into the picture. Wrestling was broadcasting live five nights a week, and the market quickly became oversaturated. Attendance began to plummet, and with it the wrestler's nightly pay outs. The wrestlers finally took a stand. They wanted television out of the picture, or they would not wrestle. Stingy promoters tried to appease the wrestlers by offering them a piece of the broadcast revenue, but the wrestlers refused. They didn't want more pay; they wanted TV gone.

Shortly before Mitchell's arrival, the wrestlers had won a temporary victory in the war. Wrestlers threatened to boycott venues that broadcast wrestling, including the Olympic Auditorium, Hollywood Legion Stadium, South Gate Arena, and Ocean Park Arena. The promoters gave in, and the box office at recent shows had more than doubled as a result of the blackout. Still, the allure of television called to broadcasters and promoters, and negotiations continued.

In late March the Music Corporation of America stepped in to broker a deal between wrestlers, promoters, and broadcasters. Under this new arrangement, the MCA became the booking agent for wrestlers in California, Arizona, and Nevada and negotiated a $50 pay out to wrestlers in addition to their take from the nightly gate. It was decided that wrestling would return to the air waves two nights a week: Thursdays from Long Beach and Friday from Ocean Park. Televised wrestling was back, but some promoters weren't happy to be cut out of the deal.

On April 17 Mitchell and nine other wrestlers walked into the Hollywood Legion Stadium and became angered when they saw television cameras set up in the building for the first time in eight weeks. The wrestlers were contracted for two television shows a week, and the Stadium was not one of the two that had come to terms with the MCA and the wrestlers. Things went from bad to worse when, instead of offering the $50 bonus per man, they were offered a paltry $48.50 to be split amongst themselves. All ten wrestlers agreed to walk out that night including Mitchell, Baron Michele Leone, Dave Levin, Chris Zaharias, Danny Savich, Billy Varga, Maurice LaChappelle, Hal Keene, John Swenski, and John Cretoria.

With no wrestlers left to appear on the show, fans were told they could pick up rain checks for the following week's show. Stadium representative Leonard Jacobsen told reporters that the Stadium would be asking the state athletic board to suspend the wrestlers.

A week later, the Hollywood Legion Stadium was forced to cancel again. By now it was clear the wrestlers would not be coming back as long as the cameras were around, and the Stadium had a television contract through May 26. Rather than fight the fight every week, Jacobsen announced that the building would be "dark," with no wrestling until after the TV contract expired.

In the long run, television and wrestling became inseparable. Promoters learned to use television as a promotional tool to drive fans to the live shows. The television program became advertising for the live shows. TV sales climbed, ratings soared, and attendance rose.

Mitchell and the other men who walked out of the Hollywood Legion Stadium were not suspended and suffered no negative blowback from the walk out. Mitchell remained a main event player, working against top tier stars like Argentina Rocca, Woody Strode, Krippler Karl Davis, Ivan the Terrible, Mr. Moto, and Baron Michele Leone.

140

Mitchell left California in mid-August, and it's not quite clear where he went from there. A Black Panther turns up on some cards in Louisiana and Alabama in September, including a match against Roy Welch in Montgomery, but there's little evidence to prove whether this was or was not Mitchell.

Mitchell did make a few dates in September in Michigan, working once again as the Black Panther. He paired with his old pal Buck Weaver for one show and in another, he participated in a multi-man match that included the man who would one day rule Detroit, the Sheik of Araby, later known simply as "The Sheik."

Mitchell traveled south to Tennessee in October, where he and Buddy Jackson of Detroit were in the "first Negro mat card ever" at the Hippodrome in Nashville. More incredible than that was a show held in Jackson, Tennessee, where Mitchell appeared in a match with a fellow African American named the Black Panther. The other Black Panther defeated Mitchell in straight falls, clinching the final victory with a neck stretcher. It's unclear who the Black Panther was, or if this was the same Black Panther who had worked Roy Welch in Alabama. Jack Claybourne was using the nickname in the Pacific Northwest earlier in the year, but any suggestion he met up with Welch and Mitchell in the South is pure speculation.

Mitchell returned to Michigan for a few dates in December before calling it a year. It's very possible he worked some dates in other states that, as yet, have not had results posted on sources like newspapers.com. Mitchell purchased - and kept - licenses for Arizona, Texas, and Montreal dated 1950, the latter two from late April.

In January 1951 Mitchell headed east to New England where he was welcomed back with great fanfare. The Black Panther made his return to Hartford, Connecticut by taking on Robert "Rebel" Russell in a 30 minute draw. He had barely settled back into a loop based out of Boston when fans were given a dream match: the Black Panther would face Connecticut's own Wild Bull Curry.

One of the most original and terrifying personas in the history of wrestling, Fred Thomas Koury, Sr., is considered to be one of the forefathers of the "hardcore" wrestling style. Bull Curry started his wrestling career around the same time as Mitchell in

141

1929 at the age of sixteen. He joined a circus wrestling show and worked as the shooter who would take all comers out of the crowd. He broke into the professional wrestling ranks in the 1930s for Adam Weissmuller in Detroit, and he wrestled into his sixties.

A well-respected officer of the law in his native New England, Bull Curry played the part of an untamed wild man in the ring. He was only six-foot tall, but he was a fearsome sight with his wild hair and maniacal facial expressions accented by the fullest, bushiest unibrow in the history of professional sports.

The much anticipated confrontation was originally scheduled for the end of January but was delayed to February due to weather and moved from the semi-main to main event in a show benefitting a local charity known as the Mile O' Dimes. The February 7 show still drew a disappointing 364 people due to winter weather, and the reported gate was only $371.75.

Those who braved the weather to see the Wild Bull and the Black Panther were not disappointed. Curry and Mitchell battled for thirty-seven minutes and fifty seconds before Curry was able to score the first pinfall. Faced with such a strong and powerful opponent, Curry was forced to do more actual wrestling than brawling, and he took down Mitchell with a body press.

Mitchell came back with a barrage of head butts in the second, determined to even the score. Curry kept escaping to the outside, drawing the ire of the fans, but Mitchell got enough licks in while Curry was in the ring to take the second pinfall in eight minutes and ten seconds. With fourteen minutes to go, Curry and Mitchell gave it their all until the sixty minute bell sounded a draw.

A week later the two were scheduled to be in the semi-main event in New Haven with women's star June Byers taking on Lillian Bitter in the main event. A crowd of 2000 packed the building to see the ladies have a go, and the show made the front page of the local paper. Most of the crowd came to see the ladies, who put on a phenomenal show, but it was Mitchell and Curry who, not surprisingly, stole the show. Fans were far more emotionally invested in the battle between the Black Panther and the wild man.

Mitchell was in good company in early 1951. Besides Curry,

other top stars working the Boston area included "Native American" stars like Don Eagle and Kit Fox, Mitchell's old ring rival Lord Blears, Miguel Torres, Tiger Tasker, Alaskan giant Yukon Eric, Chuck Montana, and "Mr. America" Gene Stanlee.

Mitchell and the others were soon joined by another special attraction. Little people, then referred to as "midget wrestlers," were becoming a very popular box office draw across the country, and stars like Little Beaver, Fuzzy Cupid, Tiny Roe, Pee Wee James, Pancho the Bull, and Sonny Boy Cassidy were soon sharing billing in Massachusetts and Connecticut. As with most special attractions, the box office saw a nice bump, which benefited everyone on the card, but Mitchell continued to be singled out consistently for having one of the best matches on the card, no matter whether he went on in the first, second, or third.

Mitchell made a debut of another kind during the summer of 1951, this time on the silver screen. A movie house ad from Racine, Wisconsin advertised a special attraction playing with the films *Lightning Strikes Twice* with Ruth Roman and *The Jackpot* starring James Stewart and Barbara Hale: the "wrestling match of the century" featuring "Mr. America" and "The Black Panther." Several such ads appeared in papers across the country with different feature films on the bill. None of the ads specifically name the competitors as Gene Stanlee and Jim Mitchell, but footage of a match between the two can be found on Youtube as part of a short documentary on the life of Gene Stanlee. Given that Stanlee is the focus and not Mitchell, don't expect to see a great deal of offense from the Black Panther.

In early August Mitchell had a clash against Baron Michele Leone. The Baron was another personality who made for a great TV star, a chiseled Italian with long, jet-black hair and a mustache who could easily have played the villain in a swashbuckling Errol Flynn adventure. Leone was one half of the card, opposite Lou Thesz, on the first wrestling show to ever gross six figures at the box office on May 21, 1952.

The Black Panther returned to West Coast in October, "from the jungles of Toledo, Ohio," proclaimed *The Los Angeles Times*. After re-establishing himself with the fans, Mitchell was booked for the

143

"first time ever" against a man he had faced two months prior and three time zones away: Baron Leone.

"Leone was never fond of Mitchell and has avoided him for over two years now," reported *The Van Nuys News* in an article that also played up Mitchell's lack of world title opportunities. "In the past 10 years Mitchell has never met a heavyweight champion. Most of the champions never wanted to face the Panther because of his unpredictable style. Many critics claim Mitchell to have more than 100 holds."

Mitchell and Leone found good chemistry together. They met again in Wilmington and battled to a 60 minute draw, tied one fall a piece. They were rematched on November 13, and it was the neck breaker of Leone that overcame the cranium cracker of Jim Mitchell.

In December the Baron and the Black Panther met again, this time before a crowd of 6500 in the Olympic Auditorium. Sadly, revenge was denied the Black Panther, and he fell once more to the hated Baron with a back cracker in the final fall.

Mitchell also had recurring matches against Brother Frank Jares, the Arizona hypnotist Dr. Lee Grable, and Firpo Zbyszko, a bald, Polish strong man with a handlebar mustache. He also worked a number of matches as a tag team with Dave Levin.

December was a milestone month for Mitchell outside the ring as well. A long-standing member of the Masons, Mitchell was granted the title of Sovereign Grans Inspector General 33rd Degree on December 22 by the Saint Joseph Lodge in Los Angeles. In the world of Freemasonry, a member can earn or achieve up to the 32nd degree, but the 33rd must be granted.

Mitchell was very proud of the honor and his association with the Masons. A number of Masonic texts survived the years in his house along with an apron, letters, special event programs, and other paraphernalia.

A Golden Superman autographed photo, from Jim Mitchell's personal collection.

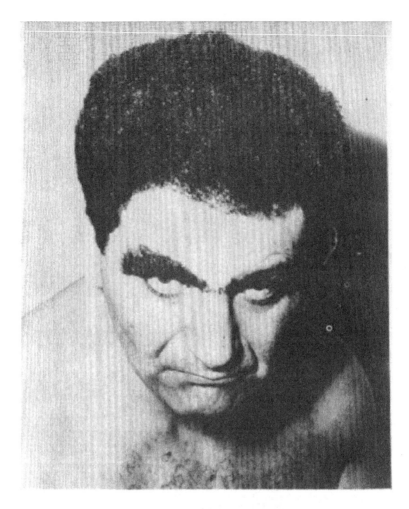

The man who invented hardcore, the wild and dangerous Wild Bull Curry.

A faded photo from Mitchell's personal collection shows the Black Panther doing battle side by side with Lord Jan Blears (lower right).

A 1950 movie ad with the added feature of the "Wrestling Match of the Century" featuring Mr. America Gene Stanlee vs. the Black Panther Jim Mitchell.

Long Beach, California program featuring Baron Leone, Argentine Rocca, and Jim Mitchell.

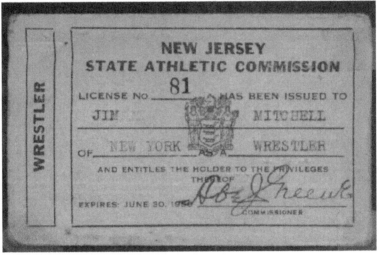

1950 wrestling licenses from Montreal and New Jersey.

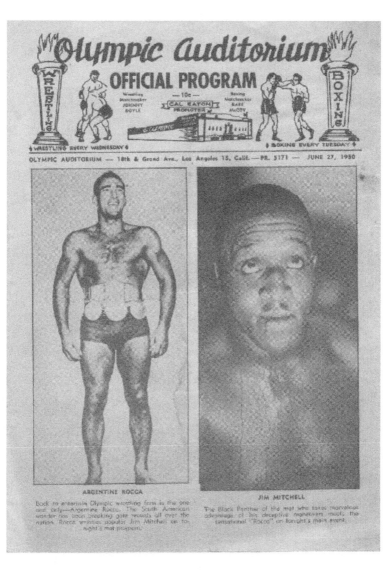

Back in California, summer of 1950.

OLYVE STUBBLEFIELD, Realtor

MEMBER L. A. REALTY BOARD

Sales, Loans and Insurance

6818 SOUTH VERMONT AVENUE

LOS ANGELES 44, CALIF.

October 22, 1951

Mr. Jim Mitchell,
c/o. Olympic Auditorium,
1801 So Grand,
Los Angeles, Cal.

Dear Sir:

Well, I was just listening to the "**Wrestling Workouts**", and heard Red Berry say that he was wrestling with you Wednesday night, and was going to drive you right through the mat. Said also that he was going to show you how to Butt heads. He bragged so much, that he nauseated me.

I sure hope you know what you are up against. You should by now know that he is a dirty, unfair wrestler. Very cagey, and knows nothing but to sling you into the turn buckle, watch out for that, and he will stomp you in the face, choke you, pull trunks, and will try the abdominal stretch on you also. He says he is going to butt yourhead until your unconscious. How about that? I do hope you will give him the worst "BUTTing" that he ever had in his life. He deserves the works, so give it to him. All Power to you. I believe you can do it, and besure and don't try to wrestle clean with that Guy. If you do he will get you sure. Show him once and for all, who can do the best "Buttin." Besure and keep him out of the ropes too.

I am looking forward to seeing you get him next Wednesday night. I think he is the world's worst, and will do anything to try to win., so besure to watchout for his dirty tricks, as he will surely try to pull them on you. Besure and butt his head so hard, that it will put him to sleep for good.

If you will just put him out, every one at our house will say "AMEN" to that. Every time he starts for the ropes, please pull him back/.

Good luck to you. We are pullin' for you, and I know a lot of people will be doing the same thing.

Yours truly,

Olyve Stubblefield,
6818 So Vermont
Los Angeles, Cal. 44

P.S. I never could see why a wrestler,—when once they get Red Berry down,—will stop. He never stops when he gets his opponent down. When he knocks his opponent down, that s when he works on him the hardest. He never waits until they get up. So don't you wait for him to get up. Jump on him when he is down, like he does, and you will beat him.

A fan letter from California, 1951. Boy did the fans hate that Wild Red Berry!

Mitchell, standing to the right of the microphone, was an active and proud member of the Masons.

THE KNOCKOUT
OFFICIAL BOXING & WRESTLING PROGRAM

JIM MITCHELL
"THE BLACK PANTHER OF THE MAT"

★ ★ ★ ★

is on

Wednesday Night's

All-Star Mat Card

at the

OLYMPIC

The Black Panther

★ ★ ★ ★

MAIN EVENT—SMITH BROS. vs. GUZMAN & TORRES

20¢   20¢

On the cover of The Knockout in California in October, 1951.

INTERNATIONAL MAN OF WRESTLING (1952 - 1954)

The Los Angeles Police Department was on high alert on January 9, 1952. On that evening, 6500 fans packed into the Olympic Auditorium to see the rematch of one of wrestling's most infamous match ups: Gorgeous George and Jim Mitchell. Memories of the previous match up from two and a half years earlier were still fresh in the minds of many fans, and most were hoping to see Gorgeous George get his comeuppance against the powerful Black Panther.

George took the first fall with a body slam, but Mitchell evened the match with a series of body tackles and head butts. The Black Panther kept it exciting for the fans, but in the end, a second body slam sealed the victory for Gorgeous George. Fans were disappointed with the outcome that night, but they kept their cool, and everyone went home disappointed but free from injury.

From one marquee event to another, Mitchell only had 24 hours to prepare for his next high level opponent, the dreaded Mr. Moto. In real life this Mr. Moto (there were a few) was Hawaiian-born Charlie Shiranuhi, also known as Young Shiranuhi and Charlie Iwamoto. He was a martial arts expert who, on occasion, would spend time with local police departments training them on hand-to-hand combat and self-defense tactics. His "judo chop" was not only a devastating finisher but the inspiration for one of Austin Powers' famous catchphrases.

Mr. Moto was known to play dirty, but Mitchell had an equalizer in the ring that night: the special guest referee, Joe Louis. Mitchell and Louis were friends outside the ring, both icons among African American athletes. Louis made sure both men played it square during the live broadcast on KTLA, and the match ended with a time limit draw.

Mitchell continued to work a number of main event matches against Gorgeous George. They met on February 23 in the Valley Garden Arena in a match won by Gorgeous George. They met again on March 8 at the San Bernardino Arena. It was unfinished business for two men who meshed well together and could draw some serious cash at the box office. The matches may have ended with draws or Gorgeous George triumphs, but Mitchell kept his stock high by winning a number of lower card battles against inferior opponents.

The year 1952 would see Jim Mitchell break new ground in two areas. After one final match in Los Angeles against Wild Red Berry in mid-April, Mitchell flew to Hawaii to work for promoter Al Karasick. Born in Bobruisk, Russia, Karasick was a ballet dancer before he sailed for the United States in 1914. He took up wrestling in 1921 and was a fierce competitor in the light heavyweight division for fifteen years, earning the nickname, the Russian Lion.

Mitchell made his first stop in Hawaii in the spring time, a trip highlighted by an Easter show featuring Jim Mitchell versus Bud Curtis in the semi-final event. The show opened with a Judo exhibition between Sally Lee and Iwalani Tanaka, and it closed with main event tag team match in which Luck Simunovich and Bobby Bruns took on Red Scorpion and Hans Schnabel. It was the "special event" on the night's card that really stood out as a historic curiosity: "Killer" Karl Davis versus the Japanese legend, Rikidozan.

Hawaii was only a brief stop on the way to an even bigger conquest. Jim Mitchell was headed to Australia.

Professional wrestling took root in Australia in the 1880s thanks in part to "Professor" William Miller, a self-described all-around athlete and claimant to the Greco-Roman heavyweight champion of the world. Miller invited American wrestling star Clarence Whistler to Australia in 1885 in order to solidify his claim to the world title. Miller lost to Whistler, but the party-hard Whistler became a victim of his own success and died in November. Conflicting reports have Whistler contracting pneumonia, falling ill from too much drink, or suffering internal damage from consuming a champagne glass. Odds are it was some combination of the three.

In spite of Whistler's misfortune, Australia became a destination for wrestlers from America and Europe in the decades that followed. Australian wrestling soared to great popularity in the

156

1930s, with fans packing stadiums to witness the action. With the onset of World War II, the foreign wrestlers were not willing to risk the ocean voyage to come to Australia, but business ticked upward once more in the late 40s and early 50s.

Ted Thye, a former wrestler turned promoter in the Northwest, was the man who booked Mitchell Down Under. Mitchell was one of a number of first timers to appear for the Stadiums Unlimited promotion in 1952. Other newcomers included Bob McCune, Gene Dubuque, Sammy Menacker, Jesse James, Lucky Simunovich, and Marvin Jones. Mitchell kept a number of pay statements from Australia, chronicling his opponents, results, and payouts from the trip. Wrestlers were paid 12.5% of 90% of the total gate, with the remaining 10% going back to the promoter.

May 3 - Draw with Bob McCune.

May 10 - Draw with Gene Dubuque.

May 31 - Defeated Killer Karl Davis.

June 14 - Draw with Sammy Menacker.

June 21 - Lost to Chief Little Wolf.

July 19 - Versus Jesse James (no result recorded).

August 23 - Defeated Chief Little Wolf.

September 13 - Versus Jesse James (no result recorded).

September 27 - Versus Marvin Jones (no result recorded).

October 4 - Versus Lucky Simunovich (no result recorded).

One of the matches Mitchell had against Bob McCune was filmed for a British Movietone news reel, and the footage can be found on Youtube. The action appears to have been played partly for laughs. Mitchell plays "peekaboo" between McCune's legs as McCune tries to apply head scissors, and some of McCune's offense sends Mitchell reeling and flailing about in a style that looks a lot like the WWF version of Hacksaw Jim Duggan. Mitchell's devastating cranium cracker is also on display in the footage.

Mitchell also participated in a benefit show for the Freemason's Hospital Association in Melbourne on July 30. The show, which raised money for the Freemason's Hospital in Australia, included two boxing matches, several vocalists, a performance by a bagpipe band and dance ensemble, a contortionist, a ventriloquist, and last but not least, a wrestling match between Mitchell and fellow Mason Sammy Menacker.

Mitchell's skill and charm earned some well-deserved press attention in Australia. One news clipping Mitchell saved from Melbourne painted a charming portrait of the man after a chance encounter on the streets, shortly after his arrival.

"One drizzly night this week I was standing in an Elizabeth Street door with Frank and Jack and Bill when we see this character coming past. They say, 'Hullo, Jim,' and he sees us and comes over.

"'Do you know Jim Mitchell?' they say to me.

"I say: 'No, how are you, Jim?' and we shake.

"We stand talking and I size him up. A quiet, mildly spoken man, easy in his manner. He wears thick glasses and easy tweeds, and smiles a big briar pipe.

"Somebody mentions the pipe. He says in his soft voice yes, he had it made in Boston from Morocco briar 100 years old. He has some 3,500 pipes, he says, some very old, collector's pieces.

"We talk pleasantly for a while, and then he resumes his evening amble - presumably before he goes back to his slippers and his fire and his book. When he is gone, I say, 'Who is he?'

"They say, 'Don't you know? That's THE BLACK PANTHER!'"

The publication *Sports Novels* ran a feature story on him in August, and the portrait the magazine paints is that of a laid back, confident man who knows how to spin a tall tale. Arriving an hour late because he was still enjoying a large lunch, Mitchell took the reporter up to his room, where he lit a large pipe and bragged about his collection of over 3500 pipes. "[They're] worth about $25,000 bucks. Guy offered it to me a few years back, too."

Mitchell told the reporter of a college football career at Texas State College and how he ran away from his hometown of Toledo at age 16 to become a wrestler in Indianapolis. He spoke about his eighteen month tour of Europe. He said when he returned to America, he won the middleweight championship from Gus Kallio and defended it against Jack Reynolds.

Mitchell told the tale about his mother giving Jack Dempsey a hook to the gut in 1937 and how the world champion still joked with him about it years later. He also spoke about the injuries he had and showed the reporter a scar on his eye - remnants of a hard thumb from Primo Carnera that required three stitches to close back in 1949.

Revisionist history and kayfabe aside, it's an interesting portrait of a man who was still enjoying himself after more than 20 years of wrestling. He noted that he owned a hotel and a restaurant back in Toledo and that his wife was owner of a coal mine. He wasn't ready to hang up the boots just yet, but he was prepared for the day he knew was soon coming. The interview ended with Mitchell heading down the street in search of his fourth meal of the day: another large, juicy steak. "What a man. What an appetite."

Mitchell discussed the hotel and the coal company in an interview with the *Sporting Globe* as well. Julia and her brother managed the coal company, Mitchell said, and Julia still found time to travel with him on most of his wrestling adventures. Asked why he would continue wrestling when he had so much financial security, Mitchell replied, "I guess the game has got right into my blood, and I love the life."

In late October Mitchell transferred his earnings from the Bank of Australia back home. He headed back to Hawaii for a few dates in October, where he worked with Dave Levin and Legs Langevin before heading back to the mainland and home in Ohio.

Mitchell finished the year in familiar territory. Not only was he back in Northern Ohio, making day trips from his home, he was raising hell with one of his greatest adversaries. On November 24 in Sandusky, Mitchell defeated Gino Angelo, the younger brother of Martino Angelo, in the main event when the referee awarded the final fall to Mitchell on a foul. Big brother Martino, who had defeated Ted Marshall in straight falls, earlier in the night, was at ringside antagonizing Mitchell throughout the contest, and the two nearly came to blows before security stepped in, breaking up the fight and (what else?) setting up an eventual blockbuster main event between two long-time enemies.

One week later the confrontation was set in Sandusky at Link's Hall. Mitchell won the first fall fair and square in 17 minutes, but he was awarded the second fall by referee Jim Scavio after Angelo refused to yield to a five count when he had Mitchell in the ropes. Mitchell was irate and began battering Angelo with head butts until blood gushed from the Italian's forehead.

Gino Angelo raced into the ring to attack the Panther while Gino's opponent for the night, Danno O'Shocker, entered to take the Panther's side. Police and firefighters were called to intervene and break up the melee, and when the dust cleared, Mitchell and Angelo were suspended indefinitely from Sandusky.

Mitchell was hardly done and hardly ready for a break. He finished the year in Northern Ohio, working a few matches in Akron.

Mitchell left behind an interesting memento from this year - his 1952 tax return. Mitchell reported a total net income of $2783 for the year, a figure arrived at on his Schedule C. His total gross income for the year was $9849, but he was able to write off expenses totaling $7029.46 including medical, massages, gym time, telephone and telegraphs, laundry, postage, lodging, and of course, travel expenses, which made up the lion's share of his expense budget. Translated to today's dollars, that amount comes to $25,707.15.

Mitchell's tax return also stated that he was away from home a total of 322 days, a very full schedule for a man who turned 44 that summer. He knew his days in the ring were running short, but he and Julia were already planning for the future.

Jim Mitchell began 1953 at home, working his old loop in Northern Ohio and Indiana as well as Southern Michigan. In January he tackled the masked Mr. X in Muncie, Indiana; Billy Sandow in Akron, Ohio; and Ted Perva in Port Huron, Michigan. He then had a date with Bull Montana II, namesake of the beloved wrestler and silent film heavy Bull Montana. The young star took Mitchell to three falls, winning the first and third with a hammerlock in a total of 27 minutes.

160

Mitchell made a long-awaited return to Lafayette, Indiana on January 31 for a 3-on-3 tag team match, a format that was just beginning to gain popularity. The ever popular Black Panther was paired with Cowboy Clay and Danno O'Shocker against villains Steve Nenoff, Mr. X, and Mr. Satan. The six man brawl was a crowd pleaser. Mitchell won over a new batch of fans with his "amusing antics and his fighting spirit," and in the chaos of battle he nearly unmasked Mr. X. Fans pelted Mr. Satan (real name Mike Ryan) with sauerkraut during the match, prompting the heel to invite those fans to "come down and see him sometime."

Mitchell defeated the denizen of Hell a week later in Anderson, two falls out of three. He received rematches against Mr. X in Lafayette and later in Kokomo. In Muncie he teamed with Billy Fox to take on Mr. X and Dutch Schultz in a tag match. Fox and Mitchell won, two falls to one.

On February 14 Mitchell defeated Doc Gallagher in Anderson, Indiana in an early match and then took a seat to watch his friend Billy Fox take on Bull Montana II. After splitting the opening two falls, Montana tossed Fox from the ring and refused to let him back inside. Montana then turned on referee Harry Burris, knocking him to the mat several times.

It was too much for Mitchell to take. He climbed into the ring and went after Montana. Montana fought valiantly, ripping off the Panther's sweater and trying to gain the advantage, but Mitchell took over with a number of head butts and knocked Montana silly. Unfortunately for Fox, and all the fans in Anderson, referee Burris recovered in time to see the Panther's illegal actions, and with the support of State Inspector Paul Ravage, he disqualified Fox and named Bull Montana II the winner.

Two days later in Port Huron, Mitchell had another run-in with the Sheik of Araby. With his play by the rules, always fair babyface image, Mitchell was the perfect opponent to put over a young, dangerous heel like the Sheik. Sadly, the good folks at *The Times Herald* in Port Huron failed to let us know just how wild the Sheik was in his confrontation with the Black Panther, but it's safe to assume blood was spilled on both sides.

In early March the newspapers of Southern California

hailed the return of the Black Panther back from his tour of Australia and Hawaii. (Sorry, Ohio.) Mitchell fell right back into the Southern California circuit, welcomed back by fans and friends alike.

Mitchell was one of a number of wrestlers selected for a special promotion with the American Red Cross. The war in Korea was on everyone's mind, and a drive was on to donate blood for American soldiers. For one week, the Red Cross in Los Angeles had a daily blood drive, offering fans the chance to get photos and autographs with top stars including Mitchell, Baron Leone, Lord Blears, Wild Red Berry, Karl Davis, Lord Layton, Sandor Szabo, Kenny Ackles, Ken Davis, Warren Bockwinkle, Dave Levin, Dr. Lee Grable, and Freddie Blassie. It all led up to an all-star wrestling show and benefit on March 30 in which Mitchell wrestled Dr. Lee Grable.

Mitchell had matches against Jack Britton, Big Boy Gardenia, Crippler Karl Davis, Joe Pazandak, John Cretoria, Ali Pasha, and Sandor Szabo. The feud over money and concerns about TV cutting into box office were long over by 1953, and television had made stars of many of Mitchell's old California friends. Mitchell made at least one major TV appearance in May when he was advertised for a match against Billy Varga in San Bernardino.

Mitchell gave an interview for an African American publication called *Sepia* that was published in April of 1953 that included some interesting family notes. For once, Mitchell acknowledged his Kentucky roots, and he said that he had built a home for his elderly mother, still alive, in Youngstown, Ohio. Mitchell talked about his son, a senior at Ohio State who was "on his way to a law degree." He also bragged on his pipe collection, once again claiming he had offers of more than $20,000 for the whole lot.

The *Sepia* article also shed some interesting light on the state of African Americans in sports. While almost all states permitted African Americans to wrestle, they were restricted to wrestle one another in the South, and never against whites. There were a few places that outright forbid African Americans from wrestling at all, including Baltimore, Maryland.

Sepia reached out to NWA president Sam Muchnick, who offered this statement: "I'm glad to get on the record on this issue. [The NWA does] not discriminate against anyone. Our laws and by-laws are designed to welcome all people and give them a fair deal... However, we are only bookers. What happens on the local level is not our fault, it is the local promoter's responsibility."

The article further noted that only twelve out of 3000 active male wrestlers were African Americans while seven out of forty female grapplers were African American. That said, even the African Americans were doing very well financially, often working several matches within a week. Spokesmen for the NWA and the Manhattan Booking Agency reiterated that the door was open for more African Americans to try the sport.

After three months Mitchell moved West again, returning to Hawaii for an extended stay. Mitchell spent most of the summer working for Al Karasick alongside notables like Hans Schnabel, Frank Jares, Bobby Bruns, Lee Grable, Ray Eckert, and Bobby Managoff.

In one of his first matches back in Hawaii, Mitchell was one of two men in a challenge match against a monster of a man named El Hombre Montana. El Hombre had 30 minutes to pin both Sonny Kurgis and Mitchell. He downed Kurgis in 15 minutes, but Mitchell survived the time limit and sent Montana to defeat. Mitchell came back to face El Hombre again in a tag match. Bobby Managoff took Mitchell's side and Mr. X - now unmasked as Lou "Shoulders" Newman of Kansas City, was Montana's partner.

Mitchell and Mr. X continued their rivalry in another tag match with two of the top men in the territory. Hans Schnabel, the new *Ring Magazine* Champion, sided with Mr. X against Mitchell and the man Schnabel defeated for the title, Bobby Bruns.

Mitchell saw some main event spots in tag matches with Bruns and Managoff, and he was nearly always a highlight on the card, renewing his rivalries against familiar foes like Lee Grable and Frank Jares. He was always just outside of the title picture, however, never getting a shot at the championship.

In September Mitchell began working his way back East,

returning to the California Coast. Mitchell's California run in late 1953 consisted of a number of opening and mid-card matches, but he had at least one marquee confrontation.

Gorgeous George was no longer a regular in his home state, having become a top draw across the country, but a new blonde villain cut from the same cloth was waiting for Mitchell's arrival. The last time Mitchell faced Tug Carlson, he was a nefarious heel who had carried his rough and tumble gimmick as far as he could take it. Unable to get his break in the main event picture, Carlson reinvented himself the same way George Wagner did when he became Gorgeous George. He took inspiration from Lord Patrick Lansdowne, donning a monocle and cape, and became Lord Leslie Carlton, a former wrestling champion of Her Majesty's Royal Navy who had come to the States to put American grapplers in their place.

On September 25 Mitchell partnered with Dennis Clary to face Lord Carlton and Benito Gardini at Ocean Park in a match televised on KLAC channel 13. It was another perfect match up for Mitchell, the long-time babyface, paired with a villain fans truly loved to hate.

Mitchell returned home to Ohio to finish the year. It was there that the Black Panther first partnered up with a young, aspiring talent named Ricky Waldo. Born in Norfolk, Virginia in 1930 Waldo stood 5'10" and weighed 240 pounds. He was an impressive athlete with a great look and a muscular physique.

Mitchell and Waldo tagged up in Indiana and Ohio a handful of times to end 1953. Mitchell saw something of himself in Waldo. Here was a chance to pass down the wisdom he had gained in nearly three decades of wrestling, to further his legacy, and to extend his own career by bringing on a semi-permanent tag partner.

After so many long years on the road and away from home, Mitchell booked a much lighter schedule in 1954. He was 45 years old by this time, and with successful business ventures blossoming back home, he was entitled to relax. Wrestling was still in his blood, however, and Mitchell was not ready to step away from the road just yet.

Mitchell made a few appearances in Lafayette, Indiana in February, putting over young stars like Paul Orth and the "Vancouver Tarzan" Zimba. He worked a handful of singles matches in Ohio and tested the waters some more by tagging up with Waldo on a few shows.

Mitchell took Ricky Waldo with him to Louisville in March of 1954, and *The Courier-Journal* made much ado about Mitchell's triumphant return home from Hollywood. Waldo was billed as Ricco Waldo from Cuba, and the new partners squared off in the semi-main event on an all-star card headlined by Lou Thesz and Mr. Moto. It was a huge opportunity for the young star to shine in front of a crowd of 9055 at the Jefferson County Armory, though Mitchell won the battle two falls to one.

By April Mitchell was on the road more but sticking mostly to his Midwest loop. He worked more tag matches with Waldo, taking on tag teams like the "Bloody" Bowery Boys. Mitchell also tagged with and wrestled against another rising young heel, Rip Hawk, who had begun his career at the suggestion of boxing champion Jack Dempsey.

On April 30 Mitchell made a one-time only appearance in Buffalo, New York for a televised match witnessed by future wrestling historian Don Luce.

"The show was the only one held at the Elk's Auditorium site," says Luce. "The Memorial Auditorium, the regular venue for wrestling in Buffalo, was booked for some other event that night. Ed Don George, the Buffalo promoter, had recently given a push to a young African American star named Bearcat Wright, who had recently scored a victory over a regular named Frank 'Tarzan' Hewitt in only 22 seconds.

"Ed Don George gave out the ballyhoo that Hewitt wanted a rematch with Wright. Hewitt started winning until losing to Wright on June 11, 1954. Jim Mitchell's job was to put Hewitt over which he did."

Mitchell was billed as a newcomer during this solo appearance, in Buffalo, but he didn't stick around after doing the job to "Tarzan" Hewitt. "Maybe the reason that Mitchell did not stick around Buffalo was because there was already a black star in Bearcat Wright," adds Luce. "Ed Don George was the first promoter to build Bearcat Wright up as a major attraction. His career took off after this."

In May Mitchell headed back up to the Northeast where he worked alongside Antonino Rocca, Yukon Eric, Sky-Hi Lee, and fellow Panther Jack Claybourne. Mitchell and Claybourne had the opportunity to work as a tag on several shows during this run in both Massachusetts and Upstate New York.

The Black Panther traveled across the border in August to work the red hot territory of Quebec. Mitchell worked in St. Johns, Sherbrooke, and Montreal. He feuded with Tarzan Hewitt, Bobby Managoff, and Jim Bernard, and he tagged with Jack Claybourne. On August 25 at Delorimer Stadium in Quebec, he wrestled Ike Eakins in front of a crowd estimated between 12,000 and 16,000, quite possibly one of the largest crowds he had ever seen.

Mitchell finished the year back home, working Northern Indiana and Ohio as the holidays approached. He worked more solo matches than tags, but he was still hooking up with Waldo from time to time. For the better part of the next two years, they would form a tag team, a partnership that would prolong Mitchell's career, and - he hoped - launch Waldo to the same level of success he once enjoyed.

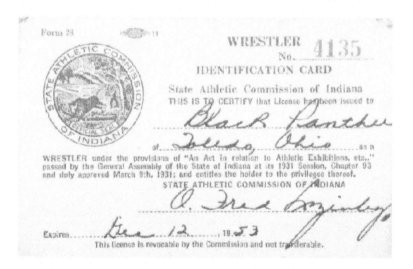

More wrestling licenses: California in 1952, and Indiana in 1953.

Page one of Mitchell's Federal Income Tax Return, 1952.

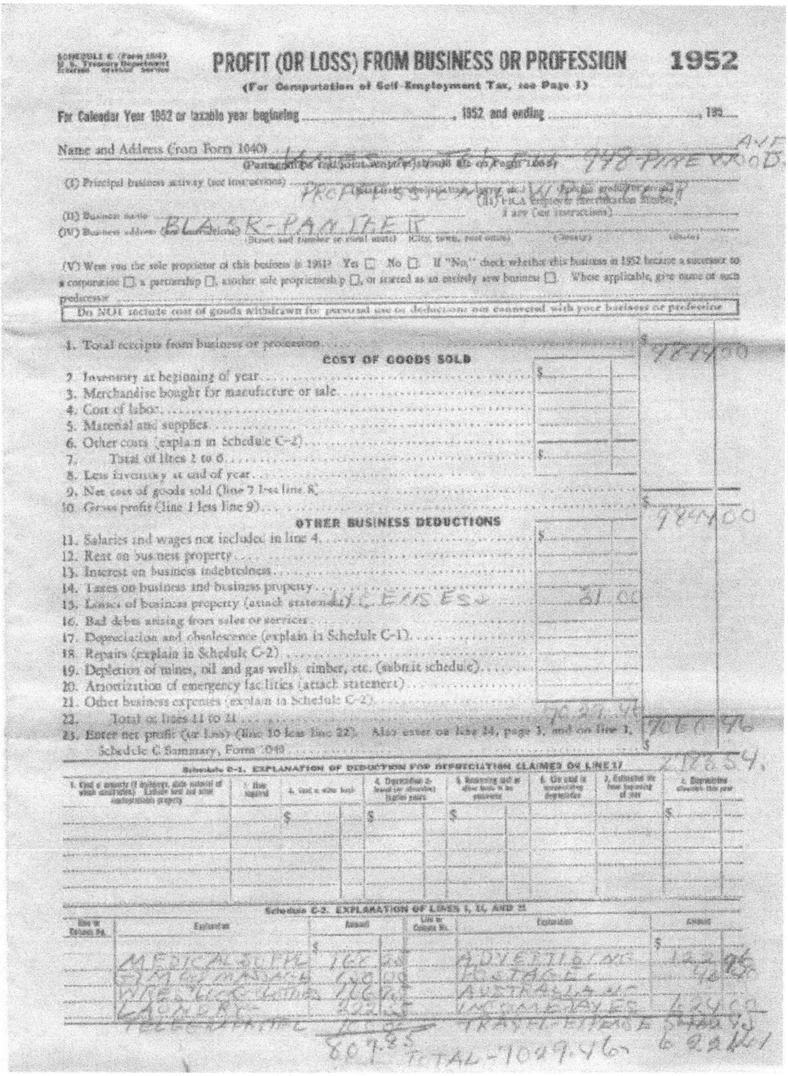

SCHEDULE C (Form 1040) U. S. Treasury Department Internal Revenue Service

PROFIT (OR LOSS) FROM BUSINESS OR PROFESSION 1952

(For Computation of Self-Employment Tax, see Page 3)

For Calendar Year 1952 or taxable year beginning ...., 1952, and ending ...., 195...

Name and Address (from Form 1040)

(I) Principal business activity (see instructions) PROFESSIONAL WRESTLER

(II) Business name

(IV) Business address BLAZER-PANTHER

(V) Were you the sole proprietor of this business in 1951? Yes ☐ No ☐ If "No," check whether this business in 1952 became a successor to a corporation ☐, a partnership ☐, another sole proprietorship ☐, or started as an entirely new business ☐. Where applicable, give name of such predecessor

Do NOT include cost of goods withdrawn for personal use or deductions not connected with your business or profession

1. Total receipts from business or profession 7844.00

COST OF GOODS SOLD

2. Inventory at beginning of year
3. Merchandise bought for manufacture or sale
4. Cost of labor
5. Material and supplies
6. Other costs (explain in Schedule C-2)
7. Total of lines 2 to 6
8. Less inventory at end of year
9. Net cost of goods sold (line 7 less line 8)
10. Gross profit (line 1 less line 9) 7844.00

OTHER BUSINESS DEDUCTIONS

11. Salaries and wages not included in line 4
12. Rent on business property
13. Interest on business indebtedness
14. Taxes on business and business property
15. Losses of business property (attach statement) LICENSES 31.00
16. Bad debts arising from sales or services
17. Depreciation and obsolescence (explain in Schedule C-1)
18. Repairs (explain in Schedule C-2)
19. Depletion of mines, oil and gas wells, timber, etc. (submit schedule)
20. Amortization of emergency facilities (attach statement)
21. Other business expenses (explain in Schedule C-2)
22. Total of lines 11 to 21 .... 7060.46
23. Enter net profit (or loss) (line 10 less line 22). Also enter on line 14, page 1, and on line 1, Schedule C Summary, Form 1040 .... 2783.54

Schedule C-1. EXPLANATION OF DEDUCTION FOR DEPRECIATION CLAIMED ON LINE 17

Schedule C-2. EXPLANATION OF LINES 6, 18, AND 21

Explanation	Amount	Explanation	Amount
MEDICAL SUPPL	168.00	ADVERTISING	122.96
GYM MASSAGE	40.00	POSTAGE	42.00
WRESTLING GEAR	166.00	AUSTRALIA INC	
LAUNDRY	327.35	INCOME TAXES	224.00
		TRAVEL EXPENSE	
807.85	TOTAL-7029.46		6221.61

How a wrestler tallies up all those deductions at the end of the year.

Program cover from Hawaii, April of 1952.

A later publicity photo of Jim Mitchell.

STADIUMS
PTY. LTD.

**AUSTRALIA'S LEADING
BOXING AND
WRESTLING
PROMOTERS**

The world-famous SYDNEY STADIUM.
Seating accommodation 12,000.

Cable Address: Stadium Sydney
Phone: FM 1361.

STADIUM,
EDGECLIFF,
SYDNEY 27-10-52 .

Also at

MELBOURNE:
STADIUM,
Dudley Street,
West Melbourne.
Phone: Cent. 7669

BRISBANE:
STADIUM,
Albert Street.
Phone: B 4164

Manager ,
National Bank of Australia Ltd.,
341 George Street .
S Y D N E Y.

Dear Sir, JIM MITCHELL

The abovenamed American Wrestler is desirous of

transferring the balance of his earnings in Australia

to the United States .

Mr. Mitchell total earnings in this country amounted

to £3873 --0--0 on which Taxation has been paid .

Yours faithfully,

Manager .

A letter confirming the transfer of Mitchell's earnings in Australia
back to the United States prior to the trip home. Mitchell kept many
of his nightly pay statements as well.

INTERNATIONAL CERTIFICATE OF VACCINATION AGAINST SMALLPOX

This is to certify that—

JAMES MITCHELL

has this day been vaccinated by me against small-pox.

CUTTER

Origin and Batch No. of vaccine _LOT # O-2236_

Signature of vaccinator _Charles J. Stein_

Official position (if any)

Place _LOS ANGELES_ Date _2-21-52_

IMPORTANT.—In the case of primary vaccina-tion the person vaccinated should be warned to report to a physician between the 8th and 14th day in order that the result of the vaccination may be recorded on this certificate. In the case of re-vaccination the person should report within 48 hours for first inspection in order that any immune reaction which has developed may be recorded.

CERTIFICATION.—I hereby certify that to the best of my knowledge and belief, the above statement is true.

[OFFICIAL STAMP]
Certifying officer
Official position _U.S.P.H.S._
Place _Los Angeles, Calif._ Date

This is to certify that the above vaccination was inspected by me on the date(s) and with the result(s) shown hereunder:

DATE OF INSPECTION   RESULT*

Signature of physician

Official position (if any)

Place   Date

*Use one of the following terms in stating the results, viz:—"Reaction of immunity," "Accelerated re-action (vaccinoid)," "Typical primary vaccine." A certificate of "No reaction" will not be accepted.

This certificate is valid for only 3 years from date of issue.

CERTIFICATION.—I hereby certify that to the best of my knowledge and belief, the above statement is true.

[OFFICIAL STAMP]
Certifying officer
Official position
Place _Los Angeles, Calif._ Date

INTERNATIONAL CERTIFICATE OF INOCULATION AGAINST YELLOW FEVER

This is to certify that _JAMES MITCHELL_

(age _45_ sex _M_), whose signature appears below, has this day been inoculated by me against yellow fever.

Origin and Batch No. of vaccine _National Drug Lab. 3304_

Signature of inoculating officer _John T. Renwick M.D._

Official position _physician_

Henry Ford Hospital

Place _Detroit, Mich_ Date _1-14-54_

VACCINATION CENTER
★   ★
★   ★
★ no. 22 ★
★   ★
U. S. A.

Signature of person inoculated _James Mitchell_

Home address _1948 Pinewood Ave. Toledo, Ohio_

N. B. This certificate is not valid:

(a) Unless the vaccine and the method employed have been approved by UNRRA, or WHO, or its Interim Commission.

(b) Until 10 days after the date of the inoculation, except in the case of persons reinoculated within 4 years.

(c) For more than 4 years from the date of the last inoculation.

Mitchell saved his vaccination records from his trip to Australia.

He also saved his passport.

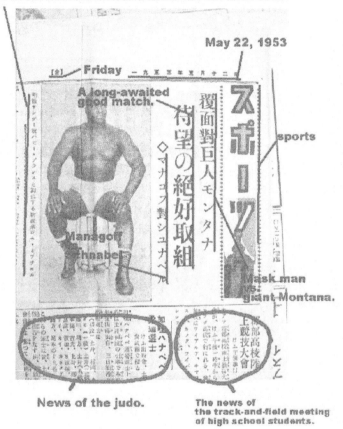

Jim Mitchell who will fight against
Bobby Bruns the day after tomorrow on Sunday.
He comes to the United States for the first time.

May 22, 1953

Friday 一九五三年五月二十二日

A long-awaited good match.

スポーツ

sports

覆面對巨人モンタナ

待望の絶好取組

◇マナコフ對シュナベル

Managoff
Schnabel

Mask man
vs.
giant Montana.

News of the judo.

The news of
the track-and-field meeting
of high school students.

Mitchell saved the sports page from this Japanese language
Hawaiian newspaper in 1953. The translations shown are courtesy
of my friend Sei Ozawa.

175

Newspaper ad heralding Jim Mitchell's 1954 return to Louisville for
the Police Benefit Show.

Mitchell posing in this undated photo with a pipe and a Mercedes-Benz SSK.

CALIFORNIA WRESTLING OFFICE

6061 HOLLYWOOD BOULEVARD

HOLLYWOOD 28, CALIFORNIA

HOLLYWOOD 9-6211

August 6, 1954

Mr. Jim Mitchell,
c/o Paul Bowser,
#2 Park Square,
Boston 16, Mass.

H'ya Neighbor,

It is nice to hear that you are still kicking around back in your old haunts. Give my regards to all the boys there--especially the booker--if you are on speaking terms with him.

Jim, it is impossible to use you right at this time as we are not only filled up but are featuring a colored boy--Bobo Brazil. You may know him.

I just returned from a trip to Mexico City--hence the delay in answering your letter. Let me hear from you from time to time.

Kindest regards,

Jules StrongBow

Jules StrongBow

JULES STRONGBOW
15650 SUPERIOR ST.
SEPULVEDA, CALIF.

A sign of the times. Mitchell was 46 when Jules Strongbow wrote this letter. His days in the spotlight were coming to an end, and the whole country was buzzing about Bobo Brazil.

"MITCH" AND RICKY (1955-1956)

Jim Mitchell started 1955 with a few singles matches, facing Bull Montana and George Gallagher among others in the Ohio and Indiana territories. At the same time, he began sending out letters, promoting himself and Waldo as a tag attraction. The opportunities weren't as plentiful as they once had been for Mitchell. He was aging, and promoters interested in an African American star had their sights set on another rising star named Bobo Brazil. Still, Mitchell was able to find some friendly territories and extend his career a bit by tagging with the younger Waldo.

In Marion, Ohio on January 31, Mitchell and Waldo worked a "Black vs. White" program with a 3-on-3 main event pitting the two of them and King Toby Thomas versus El Diablo, Herb Schiff, and Ramon Perez. All six men pulled double duty that night, with members of each team pairing off with a member of the opposite team in singles action before the big finish.

Mitchell appeared on an all-star card in Marion on March 24 facing former Ohio State football player Hardy Kruscamp. El Diablo faced Ray Stevens in the semi-main event, and in the main event, Primo Carnera faced 6'7" Len Montana - better known to movie buffs as Luca Brasi from *The Godfather*.

By March Mitchell and Waldo were billed as "colored tag team champions." They were gelling as a team, and dominating their competition. Most of their opponents were one night only pairings, as there were no other dedicated tag teams in the territory. They faced duos like Paul Orth and Danny Farrazza, Allan Stewart and Big Jim Bernard, and Tony Angelo and Red Ryan.

In May they were joined on the road by Bobo Brazil, who was already a main event star. Brazil wrestled against Tommy O'Toole, Lenny Montana, and other top heels while Mitchell and Waldo wrestled in support against whatever tag team the promoter could piece together that evening.

179

Brazil trained with Joe Savoldi, but it's likely he spent those few weeks absorbing as much as he could from the Black Panther. It is widely believed that Bobo's finishing move, a head butt known as the "Coco-Butt," was adapted from Mitchell's "Cranium Cracker."

May of 1955 was also the month when Jim and Julia purchased the property they would call home for the rest of their lives. The Mitchell's purchased the property that became 1020 Lincoln Avenue from Vergil and Ollie Baumie on May 27, 1955 for $8000. It was the house built on this location that Dave Marciniak purchased in 2002, where he discovered Mitchell's belongings, including the original purchase agreement between the Mitchell and the Baumies.

In July Mitchell headed to a new territory, the Southwestern United States, billing themselves as the Negro World Tag Team Champions. Arizona wasn't the hot bed of pro wrestling that Los Angeles was, but it presented a unique opportunity for Mitchell and Waldo. This was a chance for Mitchell to reunite with a number of old friends, a chance for Waldo to shine, and a chance to go head to head with a pair of established tag teams.

First up for Mitchell and Waldo was the brother tandem of Johnny and Jesse James. Jesse James had worked a number of territories with Mitchell in past years, including California and Australia, and the two had become good friends beyond the mat. Johnny and Jesse were the Southwestern Tag Team Champions, and in short order, Mitchell and Waldo had taken the titles away.

Mitchell and Waldo's next challenge was another dangerous pair of "brothers," the Togos. The Togo Brothers were big, powerful wrestlers with natural heat. World War II was just ten years in the past, and "Japanese" wrestlers were still natural heels, the same as "Germans." The Great Togo was American born George Kazuo Okamura from Hood River, Oregon, and his brother was Hawaiian Harold Sakata, who later became a cultural icon when he played Oddjob in the James Bond film *Goldfinger*.

The Togos were a perfect match for Mitchell and Waldo: powerful, sinister heels who contrasted with the clean, honest work of the babyface Black Panther and his young protégé. Mitchell and Waldo mixed it up with the Togos in tag matches, singles matches,

180

and even a six-man match. Waldo in particular had many opportunities to shine against some of the bigger heels, working main events as a single as well as tag team.

Mitchell and Waldo lost their title defense to the Togos after Waldo suffered a head injury. Mitchell tried to hold off the Togos, but they were too much for him alone, and they took away the titles. A week later they were given a shot at redemption. The Togos went after the already ailing Waldo, hoping to take advantage of his injuries from the week before, but Waldo escaped their clutches and clinched the final pinfall, winning the titles back for the Black Panther and himself.

Jesse James was not the only old friend working Arizona at the time. Lee Grable from California was there, and Danny McShain. Mitchell and McShain first worked together nearly 20 years earlier in Ohio and more recently in California.

Waldo received some plum singles matches during their stint in Arizona. On August 22 he worked against Dory Funk, Sr., then simply known as Dory Funk. Hard as it is to believe, there was a time in professional wrestling when there was only one Dory Funk and no Terry or Dory, Jr., involved. He also worked against the 300 pound "Manchurian" Lu Kim, who in real life was Jim Wright's brother Reuben Haz Wright, a long, tall Texan with a Fu Manchu mustache.

The newly crowned Women's Wrestling Champion June Byers made a swing through Arizona while Mitchell and Waldo were in the region. Byers was named the champion following a much debated shoot match against former champion Mildred Burke that did not go to a complete finish, but Burke's ex-husband Billy Wolfe, who controlled women's wrestling, and most of the NWA promoters sided with Byers, freezing out Burke. It was a sad end to a brilliant career of a woman who was a legitimate main event star and packed arenas across the country. Byers would not have the staying power or drawing power of Burke, and Wolfe's run as the man in charge of women's wrestling would come to an end with her reign, leaving Vince McMahon, Sr. and his chosen champion the Fabulous Moolah to corner the market on women's wrestling for decades to come.

Mitchell and Waldo expanded their travels eastward in November, making their debuts in New Mexico and El Paso, where they worked a series of singles matches against one another. Advertisements for Mitchell in New Mexico stated that he had appeared on the Rainbow Gardens TV broadcasts from Chicago. They also hinted that Mitchell's friend Joe Louis was actively campaigning for Mitchell to have a title match against the reigning (and arguably the greatest) World Champion of all time, Lou Thesz. Mitchell took a decisive victory over Waldo, thus furthering his claim on a world title match, in November.

A cartoon ran in a number of the Arizona ads, a Ripley-style feature that shared a number of facts about Mitchell including his skills on the golf course. Mitchell bragged of having a ten handicap on the golf course, and as solid an athlete as he was, there's little reason to doubt him. Mitchell put his money where his mouth was in Arizona, winning the "Desert Mashie Flight" trophy during a golf competition at Encanto Golf Course in 1955, an all-black club in Phoenix. That trophy now resides with Dr. Bob Bryla, formerly a board member of the Pro Wrestling Hall of Fame now located in Wichita Falls, Texas.

Wrestling writer Dana Raebo expanded on Mitchell's golfing prowess in one of the Southern California programs, painting a picture of a man who not only enjoyed the game, but enjoyed bedeviling his playing partners. "Jim and his deadpan expression drive his opponents on the green goofy. He is much more than a 'fair' golfer, and when he makes an almost impossible long drive right down the middle of the fairway he says, 'I just cain't seem to hit the ball like I used to.'"

Mitchell stayed in Arizona for the Christmas season, continuing to work Phoenix and the rest of the Southwest circuit. He closed the year with a pair of battles against Antone "Ripper" Leone on December 19 and 26 before finishing in early January with a few matches against the Christy brothers, Vic and Ted. Perhaps he was having too much fun to head home. Perhaps he was trying to squeeze in as many matches as he could before calling it quits. Whatever the reason, Mitchell gave the fans everything he had every week, still stealing the show at age 47.

Jim Mitchell finished his Arizona run in early January and headed home to Toledo. His traveling days were over - mostly - and life after wrestling, as much as he could stand to be away, was calling, but Mitchell would maintain a full schedule throughout the year 1956.

Most of the names had changed in the Ohio territory since Mitchell arrived in the early 1930s, but not all of them. Mitchell resumed his long-standing feud with Martino Angelo when he paired with Marco Polo to take over Martino and brother Gino in a tag match on January 24. Three nights later he went one-on-one with Angelo in Lansing, Michigan. He had a number of matches that winter against Marco Polo, Dutch Schultz, and Gypsy Bocaro, Mitchell's first clash with Bocaro in Marion, Ohio, was so violent, two referees were assigned to work the rematch.

In February Mitchell returned to Lafayette, Indiana, to face his old nemesis "Mr. Satan." The results for the February clash were not recorded by the *Journal and Courier* in Lafayette, but the match caused such a stir, a rematch was demanded and granted to the fans in mid-March with a no time limit stipulation.

Six-man tag matches were in vogue in Ohio in 1956, and that had to be a relief to Mitchell's ailing joints and bones. You would think this would be a perfect opportunity for an aging star to sit back and let the young babyfaces like Bobby Hack and Johnny Demchuck do the heavy lifting while he waited to step in and deliver the cranium cracker. But not for Jim Mitchell. The night the above trio triumphed over Dutch Schultz, Hal Keene, and Benny Matta, Mitchell also went to a time limit draw with Matta in an earlier contest that same night!

After wrapping up with the Devil, Mitchell had a series of matches in Lafayette with rising star Rip Hawk. At the conclusion of their first battle, Mitchell chased Hawk to his dressing room and staged a sit-down strike, demanding a rematch. Hawk agreed if Mitchell put up $100 as a side bet, which he did. The feud was so hot, they took their battles on to Muncie after Lafayette.

In early April a huge match was advertised in Florida featuring the Black Panther Jim Mitchell. Mitchell was billed to be facing off with his close friend, former boxing champion Joe Louis,

183

in St. Petersburg, Florida. Louis had fallen on hard time financially and had a significant tax debt to the United States government. Seeing wrestling as an opportunity to make money faster than boxing, Louis decided to try his hand at Jim Mitchell's sport.

It's unclear whether the advertisement for Mitchell was a promoter's bait and switch or whether some sort of miscommunication took place with the promoter, but the match never happened. Mitchell never made the trip, and Shag Thomas filled in. The newspaper implies that Mitchell was upset about the audience at the Southern venue being segregated.

It's just as likely that there was a simple miscommunication, and Mitchell had double-booked himself because the night Mitchell should have been in Florida, he had his hands full in Toledo. According to the *Toledo Blade* Mitchell defeated the special attraction known as the Blimp. There's not enough information in the *Blade* archives online to determine whether this was the original 600 pound Blimp or the 300 pound "Baby Blimp" who worked in Ohio later that year, but it was a monstrous challenge for one of Ohio's favorite stars regardless of which Blimp made the show.

On May 2 Jim Mitchell got a rare singles title opportunity in Marion, thanks to former rival turned Marion promoter Les Fisbaugh. Ralph Alexander was the territory champion, holder of the Tri-State Gold Belt, a title that appears to have been exclusive just to Marion. Alexander won the belt from Johnny Demchuck on April 11, and Mitchell was his first challenger. Mitchell pinned Alexander in 21 minutes with a hangman's hold, then Alexander came back and evened the match eleven minutes later. In the third fall, Mitchell turned to his signature move, the head butt, to defeat the champ and claim the Tri-State Gold Belt as his own.

Mitchell defended the title successfully on May 9 against Marco Polo, beating the young challenger two falls to one. He defeated Benny Matta the following week, setting up a title defense against Rip Hawk for the 23rd. Hawk took the first pinfall in eighteen minutes with a toe hold while Mitchell took the second with a hangman's hold. Desperate to hang on to his title, Mitchell got Hawk into the ropes during the third fall. He ignored the referee's warnings to break the hold, and the ref had no choice but to award the third fall to Hawk. Hawk got the win, but Mitchell retained the title because the deciding fall was on a disqualification.

Mitchell came back to defeat Billy Fox decisively the following week, retaining his title once again. After falling behind one fall to Frenchy Roberre in his next title defense, Mitchell came back to win straight falls and retain the title. He defeated Billy Fox a second time, two falls to one, after the Roberre match.

It was late June by this time, and Mitchell was joined on the road by Joe Louis. Louis was experiencing some financial difficulties at the time, and he had turned to the wrestling game to make some quick cash. Louis worked against Don Lee in Marion on June 27, Terre Haute, Indiana on June 29, and Lafayette, Indiana on June 30. Louis was also known to be an avid golfer, and it's very likely Mitchell and Louis played several rounds as they made the towns that week.

Mitchell defeated Ralph Alexander on the June 27 show, retaining his title once again. Buoyed by Joe Louis's appearance, the show drew the largest crowd of the year, about 1500 fans. It was also the final show in Marion under Les Fisbaugh's management. On Monday July 2, Fisbaugh announced that the wrestling programs would go on a one week hiatus. The hiatus in Marion stretched out nearly a month until a new management group was announced on July 25. The Marion wrestling programs shifted to Friday's instead of Wednesday, and none of the old familiar faces were present when the action resumed. It appears Mitchell was the last Tri-State Gold Belt Champion, never defeated for his title. Not a bad way to go out.

The Black Panther was not done yet. He continued to thrill fans in Indiana, Michigan, and Ohio throughout 1956. He faced masked mystery men and the 300 pound Baby Blimp. He tackled Prince Omar of Persia and the Elephant Boy with his ringside companion Slave Girl Moolah. He dismantled Rip Hawk once again just before Christmas.

And then, the Black Panther hung up the boots and retired. Sort of.

Odds are if you are reading this book, you are a wrestling

fan, and if you are, you already know that "retirement" doesn't always mean retirement. Jim Mitchell took the first couple of months off in 1957, but he came back to wrestle a few shows in Sandusky, Akron, Lafayette, and, if newspapers are to be believed, in Kansas of all places, working alongside old friends like Wild Red Berry and Bobby Bruns. He came back and did a few more spot shows in June in Akron before once again stepping away from the business.

All in all the Black Panther wrestled more than 30 years, 26 of those as a full-time professional. Not a bad turn for a frustrated, 140-pound teenager who just wanted to get revenge on a bully.

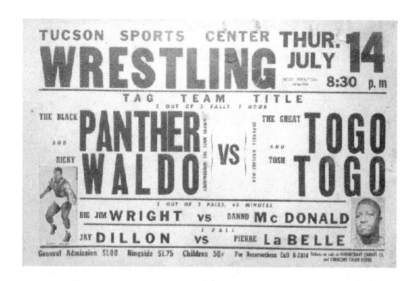

A pair of posters from Arizona highlighting Jim Mitchell and his tag partner Ricky Waldo.

Promotional photo for Ricky Waldo and Jim Mitchell, still looking fit in his late 40s.

JIM MITCHELL
THE BLACK PANTHER
LEADING COLORED HEAVYWEIGHT CONTENDER

Jim Mitchell got on the trail of fame and fortune on a bike. This was back in his youthful days in Toledo, Ohio, which is still his home town. After trying his hand at bike racing Jim used his wheel to take him to his wrestling bouts. This gave him powerful legs and building up his stamina for the long and successful career he has as a professional wrestler.

The Black Panther, which is his ring name, has met such top ring names as Lou Thesz, Wild Bill Longston, Lou Plummer, Killer Kowalski, Verne Gagne, Mike Ryan and many others. He started his wrestling in high school and the YMCA, winning the middleweight and light heavyweight conference titles and now relies on his four finishing holds which are a reverse chin lock, a crushing cracker, shoulder butt and a hangman's headlock.

Jim spends a lot of time in boys work and his hobbies are golf and pipe collecting which he has over 2000. He has a Japanese air cooled pipe of which there is only one other in the world; has pipes from China, Fiji Islands, Turkey; also opium pipes and Holland bowl pipes. These he has collected by his world tours as a wrestler, and his golf plays with a handicap of ten.

As a youth was outstanding in football and baseball and always urges all youngsters to participate in all athletic events and the best time is when you're young and always will lend a helpful hand to any youth who wants to become a wrestler and is continually addressing boys' clubs and giving wrestling demonstrations.

Mitchell is to wrestling what Robinson is to baseball and Sugar Ray was to boxing.

RICKY WALDO
225 POUNDS COLORED SENSATION
COLUMBUS, OHIO

Without a doubt one of the outstanding young colored wrestlers to enter the wrestling world today.

Ricky is creating a great deal of interest in mat circles throughout the nation * * * At only 24 years of age and only two years as a professional wrestler he has chalked up a ninety five average in the win column * * *

This 225 pound colored boy who only stands 5'9" is looking forward to a bright future in the wrestling world * * *

Ricky Waldo is a clean living athlete who came into the game the hard way and has earned his right to stay * * *

Waldo is not a college boy but is a fast thinker and quick witted and does amaze fans with his tricks in the squared circle * * *

He has a great sense of humor and is a good singer and is a past master of the piano and the trumpet * * *

Watch for this boy and you will be proud to see him in action * * *

Ricky Waldo wants to be in wrestling what Joe Louis and Ray Robinson was to boxing and what Jackie Robinson is to baseball and is fast making this dream come true * * *

Dear Mr. Promoter —

We are now booking an outstanding Colored Tag-Team Combination out of this office for your clubs.

This team consists of — first, well known and well experienced "Jimmy Mitchell" often referred to as the "Black Panther", weight 222 lbs.; second, a youthful and rising star at 24, well built "Ricky Waldo" has plenty of action and speed and has the moxie, weight 225 lbs.

Now there are various names you could tab this Colored Combination. Choose one to choose your fancy. We do believe as an all colored team they would help your clubs. Do hope to hear from you soon.

Truly yours,

Promotional flier soliciting bookings for Mitchell and Waldo.

189

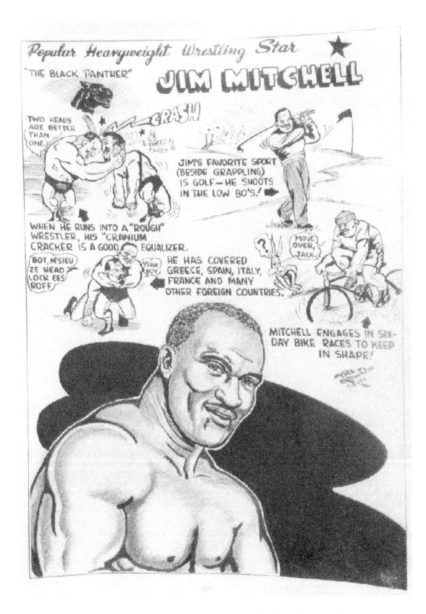

A cartoon used in Arizona programs highlighting the Black
Panther's athletic skills on and off the mat.

A gold trophy, now part of Bob Bryla's collection, Mitchell won in 1955.

ROY   TOM

We are two small men who want a chance to play on the
Amateur Show. Will you help us "pard" by buying a card?

An odd postcard found among Mitchell's things for Roy and Tom, a
country music duo featuring two men with no legs. It's possible this
was something he picked up in his travels throughout the
Southwest. Then again, a novelty act like this could probably find
an audience just about anywhere!

Above: Mitchell relaxing with a friend and a pipe. Below: A
delightfully strange personal photo of a pair of eccentric dogs from
Mitchell's personal photo collection.

RADIO STATION KNOW
CAPITAL NATIONAL BANK BUILDING
AUSTIN 10, TEXAS

PIONEER BROADCASTING CO., INC.
WENDELL MAYES, President
LOUIS R. COOK, Vice-President
and General Manager

603 E 48th
Austin, Texas

Dear Jim:

Been wondering where you were and how things were with you. Ricky came here the past two weeks to whistle and I was able to get your address from him.

After I left Phoenix and ch 3 I returned to my family here after several months of in-activity. I went to San Antonio and joined the announcing staff of KTSA. Things were going fine until about 3 weeks ago when the fellow who bought the station fired the whole staff and I was out of a job again.

Fortunatly there was an opening here at this station and I was able to land it. So I'm home with the family again — (over)

AMERICAN BROADCASTING COMPANY and TEXAS STATE NETWORKS

One of my favorite letters Mitchell kept until his death from Ed Hinkle. Be sure to note the request on page two, second paragraph from the end.

194

Playing lots golf — had a few low 10's recently and some not so low.

What have you been doing recently? Ricki say you haven't been too active of late. How about a letter catching me up on all the latest dope? —

Ricki broke the color barrier here two weeks ago and got a nice reception. He'll be on the card again next tuesday.

If youre in Phoenix again drop by the drugstore and look after my interest there. Look only!

Wife and Myra send best to you. Myra still has your picture. Its on the wall in her play room. Its ~~strange~~ strange but thats the only room in the house that doesnt have mice! — Regards to Mrs M and please let me hear from you. Best always,

Ed Hinkle

GULF ATHLETIC CLUB

502-3-4 Milam Bldg.

Houston 2, Texas

Day Phone
C. 9388-89

MORRIS P. SIGEL, Promoter

July 18, 1955

Mr. Jim Mitchell,
Rose Marie Motel,
4127 East Van Buren Street,
Unit No. 5,
Phoenix, Arizona.

Dear Jim:-

      I received your letter and publicity material
and am certainly glad that you have done so well in that
territory. Jim, we are completely over-loaded with talent
right now...and will not be needing any additional men for
quite some time.

      I would suggest that you contact me again
later in the fall...and if it is at all possible, I will
try to work you in then.

      With kindest regards and every good wish,
I am,

                  Sincerely,

                  Morris P. Sigel.

MPS:LS

WRESTLING

Letters like this one from Morris Siegel likely led Mitchell to hang
up the boots after 1956.

196

SAM MUCHNICK *Sports Attractions*

Featuring WORLD'S GREATEST WRESTLERS

Personnel

~~DICK HINDERER~~
~~Office Manager~~
RAY J. GILLESPIE
Publicity Director
DICK ESSER
Director of Ticket Sales
MARGARET NEHOLL
Secretary

Suite 230-32 Hotel Claridge . . . . CEntral 7900

1800 Locust Street • • St. Louis 3, Missouri

Office: CEntral 7486   Long Distance: CEntral 7487

July 1, 1955

Mr. Jim "Black Panther" Mitchell
Rose Marie Motel
4127 E. Van Buren Street
Unit No. 5
Phoenix, Arizona

Dear Jim:

Because of the long trip you would have to make from Phoenix to come in here for the 15th, I think it better we lay you off that date.

Sometime when you are in the vicinity, will be very happy to use you.

When we first booked you, we understood you would be in the Toledo office, which is not such a long jump.

I hope this finds you well, and that you are making money.

With kindest personal regards, I am,

Sincerely,

Sam Muchnick

SM:mn

Another no, this time from Sam Muchnick.

WRESTLING

MADISON SQUARE GARDEN — 118 N. 7th Ave.

VOL. 2, No. 26   OFFICIAL PROGRAM 10¢   PHOENIX, ARIZONA   MON., AUG. 8, 1955

The TOGO BROTHERS Put Newly Won **TAG TEAM CHAMPION-SHIP** on Line against RICKY WALDO and The BLACK PANTHER in Return Grudge Clash

Last week saw the The Great Togo and Brother Tosh win Title after injuring Waldo's leg and splitting his head against ringpost in riotous clash. Ricky and The Panther seek revenge and promise to recapture trophy.

THE GREAT TOGO AND HIS BROTHER **TOSH TOGO**
NEW SOUTHWESTERN TAG TEAM CHAMPS

RICKY WALDO SEEKS REVENGE

POT O'GOLD QUIZ TONIGHT'S GRAND PRIZE $10 IN CASH

● **ADDITIONAL PRIZE — TWO RINGSIDE SEATS TO NEXT WEEK'S MATCHES** ●

THE CLOWN'S DEN
A Sportsman's Rendezvous

MEET YOUR FAVORITE WRESTLING STARS AND ENJOY
AN EVENING OF COMPLETE ENTERTAINMENT
WITH
SMITHY 'SMITH' and his Rhythmaires
APPEARING NIGHTLY
ARIZONA MANOR East Camelback at 44th Street

Madison Square Garden
AVAILABLE FOR SPECIAL EVENTS
Contact — PIERRE LaBELLE AL 8-9014
FOR RESERVATIONS CALL AL 8-9014
Box Office Opens Monday 10:00 A.M.
Doors Open 7:00 P.M.

Arizona program featuring the Togos and Ricky Waldo.

Before we get on with Mitchell's retirement years (and post-retirement matches), I feel it's necessary to ask the question, whatever happened to Ricky Waldo? Every wrestler wants to leave a legacy, and the men and women who come after you, who were trained by you, are a huge testament to that legacy. It was always Mitchell's hope that Waldo would take his spot, traveling from one territory to another across the United States, but letters kept by Mitchell reveal that was never meant to be. Promoters who were willing to book African American wrestlers were enamored with only one: Bobo Brazil. With his athleticism and charisma, Brazil was a TV star and a natural draw at the box office. And sadly, most promoters did not feel the "need" to have more than one African American in their territory at a time.

Waldo was in the wrong place at the wrong time, in America, but he was hungry and smart enough to seek his fortune elsewhere. Details are sketchy, but it appears Waldo traveled overseas in the late 1950s, working in New Zealand, Australia, India, Malaysia, Lebanon, and Singapore, where he battled the 400 pound "Goliath of the orient" King Kong Czja. In 1960 he showed up in Japan and went straight to the man at the top. Japanese wrestling historian Koji Miyamoto tells the story:

"Ricky Waldo suddenly visited Rikidozan in April 1960. He said, 'Mr. Rikidozan, I am a professional wrestler, and have wrestled in Singapore for a few months. I am on the way back to Canada, but have no money. Would you use me for a few months? I will do my best.'

"Rikidozan agreed to use him until August 5, but he liked Ricky Waldo so much, he kept using him for two more years!!!

"The highlight of Waldo was Feb 1962. He teamed with Luther Lindsey and beat Rikidozan and Toyonobori for their Asian Tag Team championship. They were only champions for one week, but that was his highlight in Japan.

"Rikidozan again invited Waldo June through Aug in 1963."

Ricky Waldo and Luther Lindsey also made several trips across the Atlantic. A handful of newspaper clippings confirm they wrestled in the Royal Albert Hall in 1961 and in Leeds, England in 1963. Sadly, many of the African Americans who went to England to escape the racial prejudice at home in the US found similar prejudice in parts of Great Britain.

When he wasn't globe-trotting, Waldo worked for Stu Hart at Stampede Wrestling in Calgary, Alberta, Canada, where he relocated after leaving the states. Waldo and other African Americans found a warm welcome in the frigid Great White North, where Waldo won the Stampede International Tag Team Championship with Karl Von Schober.

"He was part of a group of African Americans my father booked," recalls Bruce Hart, speaking of his father Stu Hart. "There was Waldo, Don Kindred, Luther Lindsey, Big Daddy Siki, and a few others. I was just a kid back then, but when I got older, these guys told me they came to Canada to get away from the racism they experienced in the States."

Bruce was just a child when Ricky Waldo and the others made their way to Calgary. In later years, some of Waldo's contemporaries confided to Bruce that it was not only the racism of Jim Crow laws, but promoters that drove them North. "A lot of promoters would only book one black wrestler. Some big names wouldn't book them at all. I won't name names, but you can look at the cards and figure out who wasn't booking black wrestlers.

"My father was one of the only guys who would give them a fair shot. Some of them compared him to Branch Rickey with Jackie Robinson. That made me proud."

As far as Waldo personally, Bruce saw and heard nothing but good things about the man himself. "He was a big guy, very strong and athletic. A solid mid-card guy. You could tell he was half dangerous; he had a bit of a shooter in him."

Waldo's name seems to vanish after 1964, which leads many wrestling historians to speculate that "Ricky Waldo" was not his real name. It's very likely he left the business after a decade on the road, settling down in Calgary or back home in Virginia. The last trace of Ricky Waldo found to date is a 1966 trading card issued by Somportex in England as part of their "TV Wrestler" series. The card confirms that Waldo had made two trips to England and lists his confrontation with King Kong Czja as one of his most famous matches.

Whatever happened to Ricky Waldo, no one can say the man gave up on his dream. When the American promotions rejected him, he followed the lead of his mentor Jim Mitchell and forged a trail where none existed. As the Somportex trading card put it, he went "off the beaten tourist track" and made a name for himself in England, Canada, and all over Asia.

It's exciting to see the same story playing out in today's WWE-dominated business. In just the last few years, we've witness the rebirth of Cody (Rhodes), Sami Callihan, and Juice Robinson, just to name a few. They refused to settle for what "creative" had to offer, and they are forging their own destiny in other promotions in American and overseas. They refused to take no for an answer. They are making a way where none existed just a few years ago.

Wherever he ended up, whatever came of him, I'm sure Jim Mitchell would approve.

Front and back (opposite page) of a Somportex trading card for
Ricky Waldo printed in 1966.

RICKY WALDO
(U.S.A.)

Comes from Virginia, U.S.A., in the "Deep South." Will go anywhere they can put up a wrestling ring. His travels have taken him well off the beaten "tourist track" to wrestle. He's been to India, Australia, New Zealand, Malaya, Lebanon and made two visits to Great Britain. One of his most famous contests was in Singapore against King Kong Czja, the 400 pound "Goliath of the Orient."

No. 4 In a series of 60 photos

By arrangement with Dale Martin Promotions Ltd.

ISSUED BY SOMPORTEX LONDON, E.C.1

This signed photo of Ricky Waldo hung proudly in the Black
Panther Carry-Out in later years.

There were some great photos of Jim Mitchell found when Dave Marciniak bought and renovated his house. There's the very, very young publicity photo of Mitchell when he was just starting out. There are some terrific publicity pics of Mitchell in his prime and some great photos of Mitchell with Waldo. But if you want photos of Mitchell in the ring, doing what he did, you're going to have to settle for photos of the greying, balding man who just couldn't stay out of the ring, even in his fifties.

That's not to say Mitchell didn't thrill the fans as much in '63 as he did in '36. The Original Black Panther became a special attraction for the Northern Ohio and Northern Indiana fans. He was the veteran who could come in and put over an especially dangerous young heel or boost ticket sales as a special attraction.

Mitchell worked a one off show in Genoa, Ohio, on June 25, 1958, pulling double duty in a singles match and a tag. He teamed up with Herb Gerwig to defeat old friend Paul Orth and rising star Gypsy Joe, but he lost his singles match against Gypsy Joe. Yes, this is the same Gypsy Joe who, at age 72, refused to sell anything for New Jack in that horrifying match on YouTube!

Mitchell transitioned into a referee's role for a time, working as a regular and special guest referee in many of the Ohio towns where he once wrestled. Young wrestlers who had grown up watching the Black Panther suddenly found themselves under his watchful referee's eye.

"I met him doing Akron, Ohio, TV," said Jim Christy in an interview with wrestling journalist Greg Oliver. "I looked at the referee, and doggonit if I didn't know him, it was Jimmy Mitchell. I watched him wrestle out in L.A. when I was a kid."

Jimmy Mitchell, referee, was advertised as a special attractions for a few matches in Akron during 1961. On September

30 he worked Bearcat Wright versus Hans Schmidt, and on November 18 he officiated Mike Gallagher's match against the Sheik.

An intriguing article from *The Sandusky Register* teases a storyline that many of Mitchell's interviews hinted at but I could never confirm. The run down for the Thursday, October 18 show, headlined by a match between Gypsy Joe and a 750-pound bear, promotes a match between Chet Wallace and "terrific dropkick artist" Black Panther Junior, "son of Jim Mitchell." Mitchell often mentioned having a son in interviews, but there was no mention of a son in Mitchell's will or any documents found from his latter years.

Mitchell did not have any children with second wife Julia, but it was possible he had a son with first wife Ruth. The question begs, what happened to him? Or possibly, what happened between the Black Panther Senior and his prodigy? Did the son pass away? Was there a falling out? Professional wrestlers are not, by rule, model parents, even those whose children follow them into the business. And while Mitchell was known to spin a yarn or two in interviews, it seems unlikely that he would invent a son just for the sake of telling a tale.

Jim Mitchell's work as a ref led to a grudge match in 1963 against "Killer" Kowalski, the future trainer and mentor to Triple H. *The Akron Beacon Journal* hyped the hot feud for a week leading up to the Saturday, February 23rd clash between Kowalski and Mitchell. Kowalski took the victory, but not by pinfall. Instead, Mitchell was disqualified for head butting the referee out of the ring. He didn't get the win, but he went out on his feet!

Mitchell remained a fixture at the wrestling shows even after he left his role as a referee. Acclaimed wrestling historian Tom Burke has often shared the story of a missed encounter with the Black Panther.

"It was in the late 1970's, I was traveling around and found myself in Toledo, Ohio attending a wrestling card. I remember that Doctor Jerry Graham and Jerry, Jr., were on the card. I was hanging with them in the dressing room. As guys came in and out, I saw an older black gentleman talking to Martino Angelo. As I walked by I overheard them speaking about boxing and just figured that the fella was an ex-boxer."

"After the event it was off to have a few when the Good Doctor asked me if I had spoken to The Black Panther. I had no idea that the man I saw in the dressing room was Jim 'The Black Panther' Mitchell."

Jerry Jaffe, who worked as the aforementioned Dr. Jerry Graham, Jr., came along after Mitchell's referee days were over. Nevertheless, he became very familiar with Jim Mitchell thanks to his mentor, Martino Angelo. Jaffe met Mitchell in the Toledo locker room but really got to know him at the Carry-Out. Martino Angelo would make regular visits to see his friend at the liquor store, and they'd spend time in the back room spinning one tale after another for Jaffe.

"They were two very different men," says Jaffe. "Angelo was a very serious guy. His life was wrestling, and he took it very seriously. He was known for being a stiff guy in the ring, and he had a way of hitting a guy in the head that got people's attention. He didn't pop them in the ear or the jaw or anything that might have caused serious injury, but if he was upset with you he'd let you know it. George Steele really hated when Angelo would give him a shot in the head.

"Mitchell on the other hand was just a very nice guy. He had a strong, old fashioned handshake, and he was always glad to sit and talk and ask you how things were going. I really liked the man."

Jerry Jaffe told me another story about Mitchell, an incident that happened one night when he was sitting at ringside watching former rival Bull Curry.

"Bull was out of the ring and up to his usual antics, throwing tables, throwing chairs. He ended up on the side where Mitchell was sitting front row, and he gave Mitchell a shove. Mitchell stood up. He took off his hat. He took off his glasses and tossed them in the hat. He handed the hat to the guy sitting next to him, and for the next minute or so, the Black Panther and the Wild Bull had a stare down. The crowd went wild. Neither man laid a hand on the other after the initial contact, and they had everyone on their feet screaming!

"Bull finally backed away, and Mitchell sat down, but boy did they get the fans going. They never forgot the Black Panther."

An undated concept drawing for a custom robe. It's unclear if the
robe was ever finished or used.

An aged photo dated 1959 shows Jim Mitchell delivering a
"Cranium Cracker" to a foe outside the ring.

An older Jim Mitchell applying a headlock to his opponent.

WRESTLING

FOREST PARK PAVILLION

ROUTE 51 — WOODVILLE RD.

THURS, JUNE 26

8:30 P. M.   ADMISSION 90¢

GENOA VOL. FIRE DEPT. NITE

TAG TEAM Match

PAUL ORTH V **HERB GERIG**

AND

S

AND

GYPSY JOE **BLACK PANTHER**

2 Other Wrestling Bouts

– AND –

BOXING

Tickets On Sale - Green Acres - Forest Park & the Genoa Volunteer Fire Dept. Members

AUCTION SALES

AT FOREST PARK
FRIDAY 7 TO ?
SUNDAYS 2 TO ?

June 25, 1958, the night the Black Panther crossed paths with a very young Gypsy Joe.

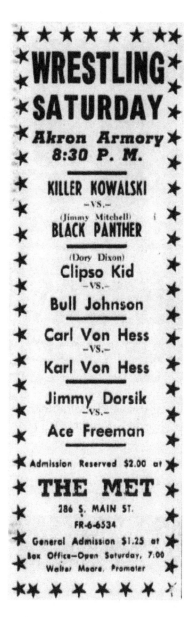

★ ★ ★ ★ ★ ★ ★★

WRESTLING
SATURDAY

Akron Armory
8:30 P. M.

KILLER KOWALSKI
—vs.—
(Jimmy Mitchell)
BLACK PANTHER

(Dory Dixon)
Clipso Kid
—vs.—
Bull Johnson

Carl Von Hess
—vs.—
Karl Von Hess

Jimmy Dorsik
—vs.—
Ace Freeman

Admission Reserved $2.00 at

THE MET
286 S. MAIN ST.
FR-6-6534
General Admission $1.25 at
Box Office—Open Saturday, 7:00
Walter Moore, Promoter

★★ ★ ★ ★ ★ ★ ★

Mitchell's final battle with Killer Kowalski in 1963.

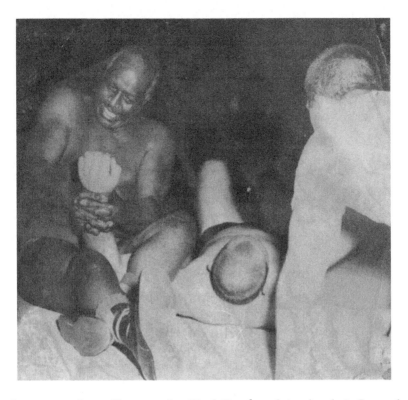

A very grey but still aggressive Black Panther doing battle in June of 1963, shortly before his 55th birthday.

Jim Mitchell with "Tiger Jack" Nelson, aka King Kong Clayton. The two men worked together on the West Coast and were Masonic brothers. This photo was sent to Mitchell in 1963, along with the letter on the following two pages that details the status of wrestling on the West Coast since Mitchell's departure.

Tiger-Jack Nelson

859½ E. 52 St.

Los Angeles, Calif. 90011

MY MOST FRIEND & BROTHER,
                              Been wanting to
contact you for a long time but I did not
have your address. You made a wise move.
   Things have fell to nothing since you and
   all the real boys out out. we have nothi
   but Long Beach,Olympic,Bakersfield,
San Diago, (some times)because we have
Tijuana and thats on T.V. the next night so
so San Diago house is down because thexpaa
people see everything on T. V. Oh yes we d
   do have San Bernadino. That is all we
   have out here. Johny Doyl has all of the
   teritory in Australia & europe. Promotes
nothing but spot shows. Jules Strongbow is
   the big man out here now and a great mam.
   to the men.(also MR. Moto is the big man
Mike Hirsch, Sandor Szabo , is out of the
buisness. (permantely).. I mean (OUT)..
   The programs is not like their were
   when you & the old gang were here. all
   the old gang is retired, Dr. Lee Grable
   the Snable brothers,Dutch Hefner, Pat
Fraley & so many outhers is working at
some U.S. secrets plant for the govt.
   They dont come around us anymore.
Baron Leone is in the apt. house
buisness.(he quit)Cal Eaton Died.Herby
Freeman died. Sammy Stien died. Jules
   Strongbow, has had 3 strokes but is all
right now.Bobo Brazil worked here last
   night.He told me that you asked about me

And said you told him what a swe,11 man you
thought I was. Oh yes Pasadena is no more
Murry Cohan sold the building. So he told
the office t.at he owed all the money he colected
and he had to have momey yo pay rent to maintain
the place so the boys could have a place to wres
wrestle. So Jules (the office) gave him the
money to pay the rent so he could have a place
for the boys to work. Murray took the money
and put it in his pocket and did not pay the
man so the owner closed the building because
Murray run 18 shows and did not pay the rent.
The owner tore the building down it is a parking
lot now. Oh yes, Our old Friend Harry Rubin,
Is handleding women entertainers in Las
Vagas (two of them). He has two strokes. He
is all right now. My two daughters(indirectly)
sends their regauds t o you.They are on the
board of education here in L.A. Bobo girl Friend
my outher (foster daughter)is working in a bank
in N. Y.. she had a fine boy by him. Mike Hirch
is out of the picture. Let me here from you I
have so much to tell you.
 FROM YOUR TRU AND TRIDE FRIEND,
 TIGER JACK NELSON. (THEODORE ROOSEVELT REED)

4/19 '63

Hello Panther;

Its been along time since we got together and alot of things have changed,first I was married 40 years before she decided she did'nt want me anymore and left(why I still don't know)well anyway I'm married again and I hope this one lasts for 40 years and I'll be satisfyed.Then at 55 years old I had to go out and look for my first job and beleive that is'nt at that age,I think I did a little of about everything until I decided to take this Guard Job and here I have been for going on 7 years.One thing nice,every week I get a chech and I'm not writing them when I did'nt know where the money was coming from and the wrestlers would'nt listen to me.

The girl at the Credit Union told me about you stepping in and gave me your address,wish we could get together sometime,we have a nice home here on Catawaba Island and when I get 65 years old I'm going to tell them all to kiss my ass;I've had it.I&ll give you my address add draw you a map on how to get here,hoping to see you in the near future

As Always

Les Fishbaugh   Phone 797-2212
Rt.1 Box 251
Port Clinton,Ohio

A letter from old friend Les Fisbaugh, 1963.

While working on this biography, one set of artifacts found in Jim Mitchell's house took on a life of their own. Some great discussion happened on social media as I tried to puzzle out the purpose of these items, and after some collaborative detective work, we solved the mystery.

After my second trip to Toledo, I found a handful of faded, water-damaged note cards and papers stuffed away in a leather case. Written on these documents were the cards for the weekly Toledo wrestling shows from summer 1962 through spring 1963. It seemed strange that Mitchell would have kept these cards from a time when he was no longer actively wrestling, and as I shared the cards with other wrestling enthusiasts, including Mark Henry and Brian Last, the question that soon came up was this: could Mitchell have been booking these cards?

It was a question that needed to be pursued as far as possible. If Mitchell was indeed booking, he would likely have been the first African American booker in American professional wrestling, pre-dating Ernie Ladd by more than a decade.

I showed the cards to Jerry Jaffe, since Martino Angelo was the booker of record in Toledo during this time, but he had no first-hand knowledge of Mitchell's involvement. I then posted the cards on a few Facebook pages at the urging of Brian Last, and we soon started to get some more pieces to the puzzle.

A close examination of the handwriting by Jason Campbell showed that the handwriting was not the same on all the papers. I was able to match a few cards to other samples of Mitchell's handwriting (specifically, his 1952 tax return), but the others were clearly written by someone else.

Tim Hornbaker chimed in and informed me that the Toledo office was booking wrestlers through Fred Kohler's office in

Chicago and the Barnett/Doyle office in Indianapolis. This matches with the letterhead on one of the papers bearing the Toledo wrestling cards. Hornbaker suggested Mitchell might have had a small role in coordinating between Angelo and the larger booking offices, but he would not have been booking the actual matches. This all but shut the case on whether Mitchell was booking, but it didn't tell us what the cards were for.

We needed to find someone who had first-hand knowledge of Angelo's promotion, and I was put in touch with a former wrester named Terry Sullivan. Terry had no knowledge of who made the matches in Toledo in 1962-1963, but after looking at the cards, he suggested Mitchell may have been taking the finishes between the locker rooms. The heels and babyfaces dressed in the hockey locker rooms at opposite ends of the Toledo Sports Arena, so someone would have to run the finishes between the two. The problem with this theory is that there are no tick marks over any names to indicate who was going over.

Sullivan then proposed another theory: Mitchell may have been delivering the cards to the local newspaper so they could prepare the weekly ads. He noticed that the card for November 7, 1962, had the word "Pict" written beside two names, Art Thomas and the Mongol, and each note had different days of the week noted as well. Sunday and Wednesday were noted next to Thomas, and Tuesday was noted beside the Mongol.

Sullivan said that when he was wrestling in Toledo, Angelo personally delivered the cards to the newspaper. Since Mitchell was such a trusted friend, it's conceivable Angelo could have had Mitchell make the weekly stop by the newspaper with the cards. This not only accounts for the cards being in Mitchell's possession, but for the various handwriting samples. Sometimes Angelo would write the cards down, sometimes Mitchell, sometimes someone else connected to the promotion.

Sullivan and I checked the cumbersome online archive of the *Toledo Blade*, but we did not see any wrestling ads during the week of the November 7, 1962 show. Sullivan then told me there used to be another newspaper called the *Toledo Times* that was released in the mornings while the *Blade* came out in the afternoon.

The *Times* had a smaller geographical circulation than the *Blade*, and the ad rates would have been lower. Unfortunately, the *Times* has been gone for decades, and there's no online archive at all.

Enter Marcus Everett.

For those who don't follow modern independent wrestling, let me refresh your memory. Marcus is the guy from that GIF you've all seen jumping off a wall and overshooting a table at the former IWA Mid-South Arena in Memphis, Indiana. Yes, he's THAT guy. Marcus is also a very sharp, well-read fellow who, like me, has more books stacked up around his house than he can ever possibly read. The old saying, "Don't judge a book by its cover," certainly applies here.

Marcus lives in Toledo, so I asked him if he would mind swinging by the library to check the microfilm archives. He was eager to give it a shot, so he set an appointment with the library to search through the *Toledo Times* archives.

After a brief false start (my fault, as I gave him the wrong year at first), Marcus hit pay dirt. In the Sunday, November 4, 1962 edition of the *Toledo Times*, he found "Seaman" Art Thomas's photo with the wrestling ad.

As exciting as it would be to say Mitchell was the first African American booker in history, it was still a thrill to uncover the purpose behind these mystery cards. This conclusion doesn't mean Mitchell wasn't in some way contributing to the booking of the shows, but it's another tiny clue to his days after wrestling. Like so many men before and after him, Mitchell never got the business completely out of his blood.

A sample of the cards are printed on the following pages, along with the newspaper ad that closed the case.

FRED KOHLER
Enterprises INC

817 WEST GRACE STREET · CHICAGO 13, ILLINOIS

WEllington 5-2218

TOLEDO, OHIO   WED. SEPT. 26

BAVARIAN } vs. { BAREND John + #0
BOYS   { MAURICE Crystals

JEAN LANE vs. BERNICE LARUE

JACK WILSON vs. PAUL CHRISTY

BILLY ROLLING THUNDER vs. LEE ANDREWS

TOLEDO
FEB 13, 1963

THE SHEIK vs KIT FOX

THE MONGOL vs AL TORRES

CZAYA NANDOR vs BOMBA

NICOLAI VOLKOFF vs RAMON TORRES

Jan 7 - 1963

Bill Miller
vs
Czaya Nander

The Sheik
vs
Mark Lewin

Tag Match

Torres Bros vs N. Volkoff Rudy Kay

Don Jardine
vs
Don Leo Jonathan

P. LaBelle
vs
The Mongol

Toledo Feb 20 1963

Bill Miller
vs
Bearcat Wright

Girl Tag Team
Brenda Scott
Judy Grable
vs
Rita Martinez
Ann Casem

Ramon Torres
vs
The Mongol

Nicolai Volkoff
vs
Joe Blanchard

Feb 20th

GIRL TAG TEAM MATCH

Judy Grable
and
Linda Scott
vs
Rita Martinez
and
Patty Casey

Bill Miller vs The Mongol

Ramon Torres vs Joe Blanchard

Bearcat Wright vs Nicolai Volkoff

223

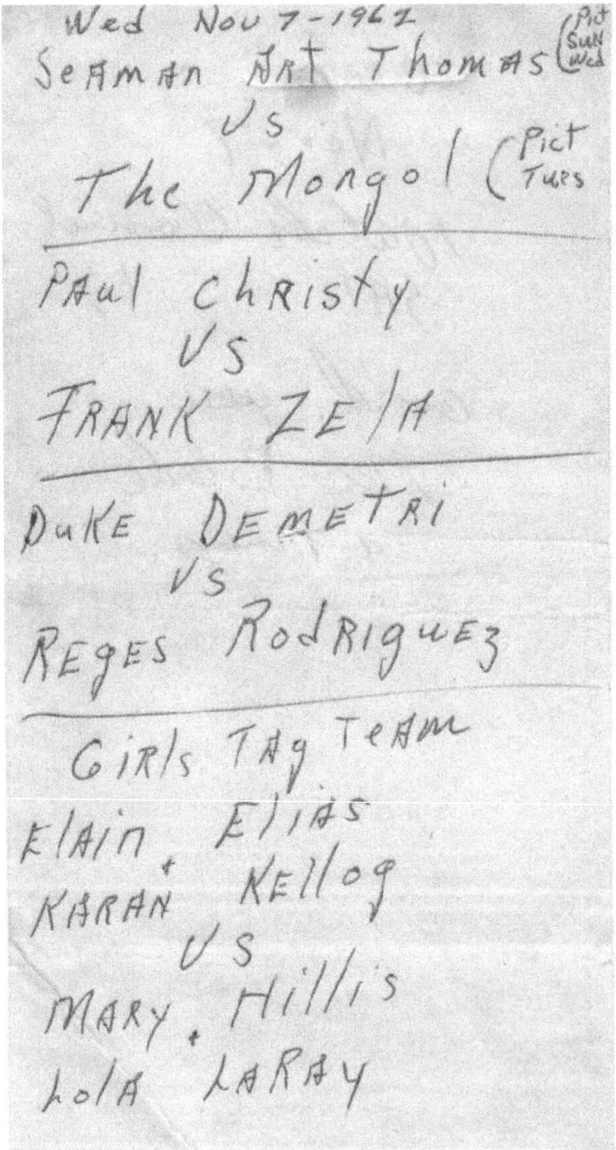

Wed Nov 7-1962

Seaman Art Thomas (Pict Sun Wed)

vs

The Mongol (Pict Tues)

Paul Christy

vs

Frank Zela

Duke Demetri

vs

Reges Rodriguez

Girls Tag Team

Elain Elias
+
Karan Kellog

vs

Mary Hillis
+
Lola Laray

The "Rosetta Stone" card. See the notes next to Art Thomas and the Mongol's names…

And here's the ad featuring Art Thomas.

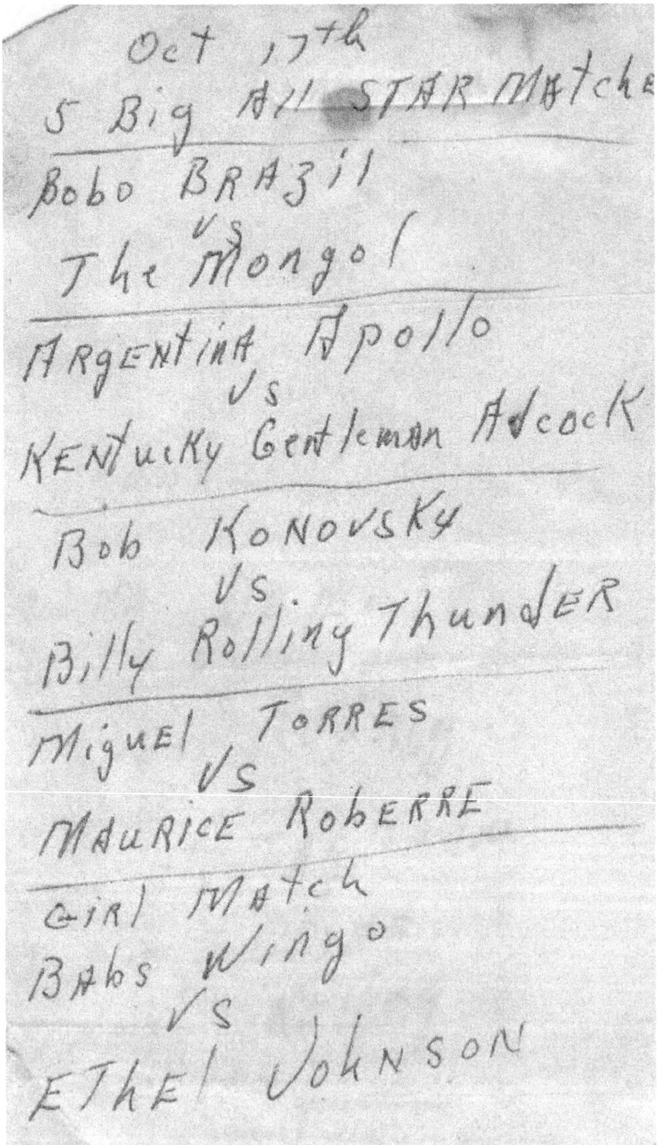

Oct 17th
5 Big ALL STAR Matche

Bobo BRAZIL
vs
The Mongol

Argentina Apollo
vs
Kentucky Gentleman Adcock

Bob Konovsky
vs
Billy Rolling Thunder

Miguel Torres
vs
Maurice Roberre

Girl Match
Babs Wingo
vs
Ethel Johnson

If you search for 1215 Dorr Street in Toledo, Ohio on Google Maps, you are going to be in for some disappointment. There's a vacant lot where the Black Panther Carry-Out once stood, and that vacant lot is representative of what happened to much of the historic street once known as Detroit Avenue.

At the time Jim opened the doors of the Carry-Out, Detroit Avenue was a lively place, a proud African American community. Dorr Street was named after Toledo's 10th mayor Charles Dorr. It was a largely residential area, with some homes dating to the early 20th century, but a number of well-known businesses fronted Dorr, especially along the 1200 and 1300 blocks where Mitchell's store was.

A few doors down from the Carry-Out was the Theater Bar, owned by Texans Samuel and Leatrice Griffin. Septa Enterprises sat at 1229-35 Dorr Street and owned by an attorney named Theodore Gerz. The building was split between a storage facility and a restaurant, Dorr Luncheonette.

Giant Supermarket sat at 1241-1243 Dorr Street until 1974. The block was sold to Archie Smith and Jim Billups, who owned an appliance store down the street. They renamed the shop Jimmy's Carry-Out.

Miller's Hardware was at 1245-49 Dorr Street, operated by Virgil Miller. Roland's Credit and Jewelry was located at 1253-55 Dorr Street. The Lincoln Motel was at 1259-61 Door Street, operated by Curtis Goode and Clarence Spearman. A small restaurant was also part of the 33 room property.

Seaport Mold and Casting had a manufacturing plant on Dorr Street. Owen Moore owned and operated Moore's Barbershop. Dorr Cleaners and Laundry was located at 1307 Dorr Street. The Be Square Club was at 1327 Dorr Street. Clark's One Stop Record Shop, owned by Fred and Ednah Page, was at 1315 Dorr Street and offered free delivery.

A few churches were also located on the strip. Thomas Temple Church of God was located as 1244-46-48 Dorr Street, and the Jesus Only Church of Deliverance was at 1305 Dorr Street.

Gilbert and Mayme Turner owned the hot spot on the block, a place known as The Spot at 1344 Dorr Street. Their son Nelson managed the restaurant and bar for them. Another popular hangout was the M & L Rendezvous Bar, which was shut down in 1973 after a judge ruled the place to be a public nuisance.

Mitchell had owned and operated several businesses during his wrestling career, going back to the barbecue restaurant he opened in 1940. He also made mention of a hotel and night club back in Toledo. Long before he met Jim Mitchell, a curious Jerry Jaffe paid a visit to a club called Black Panther in an African American neighborhood.

"This was a really turbulent time in Toledo as far as race. I was the only white person in the building, and no one would even pay attention to me. I asked if a wrestler still owned the place. They wouldn't answer. No one took my drink order either. They probably thought I was a cop. They didn't try to kick me out or tell me to go away, but I eventually got up and left. I later heard that Mitchell had sold the place prior to my visit, but yeah, he did have a night club at one time."

When Mitchell decided to call it a career in the ring, the Carry-Out became his new full time endeavor. The sign outside the shop included a portrait of Mitchell in his prime, wearing his wrestling trunks and boots. Neighbors, passersby, curious visitors, and wrestling fans loved to step inside the shop at 1215 Dorr Street to gaze on "Panther's Gallery," a wall covered with promotional pictures of wrestlers Mitchell had known and worked with.

Panther's Gallery was preserved in a small snapshot kept by Mitchell. What's amazing is that most of the photos from the Gallery survived the years and were found in his home: Bobo Brazil, Ricky Waldo, Vern Gagne, the Volkoffs, the Mongol, the Gallaghers, Kit Fox, Carl Engstrom, and Moose Cholak, just to name a few.

Mitchell never minded when people stopped in just to talk. He loved to tell stories from his wrestling days, and he kept it kayfabe for the fans. When fellow wrestlers would drop in, things were a bit different. Mitchell would invite special guests like Bull Curry and Martino Angelo into the back room. He would break out the "good stuff," and they would share the real stories of yesteryear. Angelo's pupil Jerry Jaffe and Curry's son "Flyin' Fred" Curry were both privileged to come along on some of these visits and hear stories about the old days.

"Sometimes the issue of race would come up," says Jerry Jaffe. "Mitchell would talk a little about the Jim Crow laws, the states where he was unable to wrestle because of his skin color, but he didn't say much about it. I'm sure he had his share of problems, but he never spoke much about it. He wasn't the kind of person to let things like that get him down. He was the kind of guy who overcame those obstacles. He was also the first black man to wrestle a white man in the state of West Virginia. He was very proud of that. He was proud of his legacy, proud of the things he accomplished in spite of the times."

Step-daughter Roberta Conn spoke about Mitchell's response to the Black Panther in the late 1960s. "He was the Black Panther before all that mess was even thought of. Before he ended the business, he changed the sign and called it the 'Original' Black Panther Carry-Out, as if there would be two. We laughed at that."

Mitchell added to his legend with an incident that took place at the Carry-Out one evening in 1971. According to the police report, a man with a sawed-off shotgun walked into the store around 11:30 p.m. and demanded the cash from the register. When Mitchell failed to answer, the would-be thief said, "I'm not kidding. This is a stickup!"

Mitchell responded by stepping toward the gunman and grabbing the shotgun, yanking it out of the intruder's hands. The man fled.

Even at age 62, the Black Panther was no one to be trifled with!

"Panther's Gallery" inside Black Panther Carry-Out, a wall featuring a who's who of professional wrestling. Pictures above include Joe Louis, Ricky Waldo, Verne Gagne, the Gallaghers, Kit Fox, and Bobo Brazil.

Business cards and a matchbook from the Carry Out.

Above: A cigarette dealer's license from the Carry Out. Below:
Julia's 1984 driver's license.

Above: Julia holding a child (grandchild?) in front of the Carry-Out.
Below: Jim and Julia outside the store.

A golf permit and a handgun permit, both belonging to Jim Mitchell.

Mitchell's pride and joy was his pipe collection, once valued at over $25,000. Some personal photos of his more unusual items are shown above.

A small sampling of Mitchell's pipe collection, photographed in
2017

An ornately carved pipe (above) and a coconut with a corncob pipe (below) sitting atop one of Mitchell's travel cases.

Mitchell kept a few pieces of art work depicting him enjoying his favorite pasttime.

A sketch Mitchell received during his Australia tour, 1952.

Jim Mitchell lived a very public life for almost thirty years. He traveled the world. He became a fan favorite in every territory he worked. He planned well for the future during his heyday, and when his time was up, he faded away gracefully, making way for the generation that followed.

By the mid-1960s, Mitchell transitioned from a very public life to a largely private one. He remained active in the Masons and other civic endeavors, and he continued to take in wrestling in Toledo, but his life and adventures were no longer the stuff covered by the sports pages.

In other words, as much as I'd love to tell you about his post-wrestling life, his marriage to Julia, his relationship to his step-daughter Roberta, and the happenings on Dorr Street and Lincoln Avenue, there's not much I can tell.

Mitchell was said to do a lot of work with young boys during his wrestling days, and it's likely this carried over into his post-wrestling life. Mitchell always expressed gratitude for the opportunities afforded him, and he didn't mind being put up as an example of someone who worked hard to rise up from his humble beginnings.

Mitchell's pipe collection continued to be a hobby as well, and he loved to brag on some of his rarest treasures. He claimed to have a very rare Japanese air-cooled pipe, one of only two existing. He had pipes from China, Turkey, and the Fiji Islands as well as opium pipes and Holland bowl pipes. Mitchell's newspaper clippings included a few articles about pipes and pipe smoking including one about a pipe smoking contest sponsored by the International Association of Pipe Smokers Clubs.

In 1973 *Wresting Revue* magazine ran a "Where Is He Today?" article on Mitchell. Alongside a vintage photo of Mitchell in his prime and a photo of Jim and Julia in front of the Carry-Out, the article gave Mitchell credit for being one of the first black wrestlers to work main events and put over his early practice of riding his bike to make towns. Said Mitchell, "The Indianapolis to Cincinnati trip was a boring ride."

Mitchell loved when people dropped by to check out the "Panther's Gallery" of photos on the wall, and he loved to tell stories. After posting a brief biography of Mitchell online, several former residents of the Dorr Street neighborhood reached out to me to tell me how kind he was and how much he loved showing off his photos and spinning tales of his life in the ring. Jim Mitchell was proud of his legacy, and he never minded when someone dropped in not to shop, but just to listen.

Mitchell kept shop at the Carry-Out until 1982, when the building was sold to the city by the Toledo Paper Box Company, the building's owner, to the city of Toledo, for $23,500. Mitchell had leased the property from the owners for many years, and as a concession, he was paid an additional $6,845. It was a pittance, even for the time, and typical of the buyout offers extended to other property owners all along Dorr Street. Still, Mitchell was more fortunate than many of the other shopkeepers who rented or leased their space.

The city of Toledo bought out most of the owners on Dorr Street in 1982 in an effort to clean up the neighborhood. While the state of Ohio and the city of Toledo invested in many neighborhoods as a way to revitalize certain areas, Dorr Street received no special investment. Much of the neighborhood was demolished, including the Carry-Out. As of 2017 the street bore little resemblance to the thriving "Detroit Avenue" community of yesteryear. Visitors will find a few businesses, some apartments, a couple of gas stations, a fire station, a library, a restaurant, and a large number of vacant lots where a thriving community once dwelled.

Mitchell was 74 when the Carry-Out was sold out from under him. His wife Julia was 82.

Six years after the Carry-Out closed, we get our next peek into their later years. In 1988 Mitchell revised his will for the final time. Julia was named his sole heir, and in the event of her passing, Roberta was to receive everything.

Again, one has to wonder if there ever was actually a son, and if so, what had become of him by this time?

The Mitchells also signed over ownership of the house at 1020 Lincoln Avenue to Roberta, who was taking mail at that address. Dave Marciniak found suitcases and papers belonging to Albertus B. Conn, Julia's first husband and Roberta's father, inside the house along with Mitchell's things. Roberta most likely moved into the house at that time to care for her aging parents.

It's very likely that both Jim and Julia were in failing health by this time. Mitchell suffered from Alzheimer's and later cancer, which took his life. These two small steps taken at age 80 were most likely final preparations for the day when he would no longer be able to make decisions for himself.

In 1990 Mitchell was admitted to Northfield Place Nursing Home in Whitmore Lake, Michigan, an hour north of Toledo. Although there's no evidence to support it, it's very likely his 90 year old wife went with him.

On August 10, 1994, Julia Mitchell passed away. Her obituary listed her as a native of Toledo and owner of the Harter Coal Company founded by her father in 1905. She was a graduate of Scott High School and attended Wilberforce College. She was also a member of the Warren A.M.E. Church, and of course, wife of the former professional wrestler once known as "The Black Panther."

Two years later, Mitchell passed away at the nursing home in Whitmore Lake on June 19, 1996. A simple obituary ran in the *Toledo Blade*, and a longer article appeared on the opposite page.

Roberta Conn gave an interview for the story. She described her stepfather as a strong man who never let on when he was in pain, whether in the ring or out. She talked about his love of the business and how he traveled mostly by car and mostly by himself for so many years. "It wasn't a bad life at all. He liked it, and the people liked him."

The article listed Roberta as his only survivor and gave time and dates for visitation at the Dale Funeral Home in Toledo. He was buried next to his beloved Julia in Woodlawn Cemetery.

Roberta remained in the house on Lincoln Avenue until her death on November 5, 2002. It was shortly after that Dave Marciniak purchased the house she had called home with her mother and stepfather for so long. In the house Marciniak not only found items belonging to Jim Mitchell but to Julia, Roberta, and Albertus B. Conn, Julia's second husband and Roberta's first stepfather, whose last name she had taken for her own. Albertus had passed away in 1949 at the age of 44.

Last Will and Testament

of

JAMES MITCHELL

KNOW ALL MEN BY THESE PRESENTS: That I, JAMES MITCHELL, of Toledo, Ohio, being of sound mind and memory, and of full age, do make, publish and declare this to be my Last Will and Testament, hereby revoking any and all Wills by me heretofore made.

ITEM I

I direct that all my just debts and funeral expenses be paid out of my estate as soon as practicable after my decease.

ITEM II

All of my property, both real and personal, of every kind and description and wheresoever situate, which I may own or have the right to dispose of at the time of my decease, I give, devise and bequeath to my wife, JULIA E. MITCHELL, absolutely and in fee simple.

ITEM III

In the event my wife, JULIA E. MITCHELL, predeceases me, or in the event we die in a common casualty, I give, devise and bequeath all of my property, both real and personal, and wheresoever situate, and of every nature whatsoever, to my step-daughter, ROBERTA B. CONN, absolutely and in fee simple.

ITEM IV

I hereby nominate and appoint my wife, JULIA E. MITCHELL, as Executrix of this my Last Will and Testament and direct that no bond be required of such Executrix. I direct that my said Executrix shall have full power, at her discretion, to make sales of all or any part of my estate, at public or private sale, without order or confirmation of court, and upon such terms and conditions as she may deem advisable; to compound, compromise or otherwise settle and adjust any and all claims, debts or demands of any description against or in favor of my estate; to execute contracts, releases, deeds, proxies or any other instrument or document relating to my estate and its administration, and to do any and all acts or things necessary and proper to the complete administration of this my Last Will and Testament.

IN WITNESS WHEREOF, I have hereunto set my hand at Toledo, Ohio, this   day of   . 1989.

—————————————————————————
James Mitchell

The foregoing instrument was signed by the said JAMES MITCHELL, and by him acknowledged to be his Last Will and Testament, before us and in our

Original in the possession of Keipp & Weingart Co, C.P.A.

A copy of Mitchell's will, leaving everything to Julia and then Roberta.

245

NEIPP & WINGART
A Legal Professional Association
ATTORNEYS AT LAW
627 MADISON STREET
TOLEDO, OHIO 43604
AREA CODE 419
473-1411

R. PAUL WINGART
WILLIAM H. BRAULT
JOHN T. KEHL

KATHLEEN W. STRIGGOW
MARK D. EDWARDS

OF COUNSEL

October 12, 1988

James Mitchell and Julia E. Mitchell
c/o Roberta B. Conn
1020 Lincoln Avenue
Toledo, Ohio   43607

Dear Mr. and Mrs. Mitchell:

Please find enclosed the Deed to the property located at 1020 Lincoln Avenue which has now been recorded with the Lucas County Recorder.

I have also enclosed my statement for services rendered in preparation of the Deed and Wills for James Mitchell and Julia E. Mitchell. Please feel free to contact me should you have any question whatsoever after reviewing the enclosed documents. My thanks for the opportunity to serve your interests.

Very truly yours,

Kathleen W. Striggow

KWS/lcm
Enc.

Aging and in poor health, Jim and Julia Mitchell signed their home over to Roberta Conn, Julia's daughter, in 1988.

Form--4.0   11.82   Legal News, Toledo, Ohio

After recording mail to:
Kathleen Striggow, Attorney
4127 Monroe Street
Toledo, Ohio 43606

QUIT-CLAIM DEED (Statutory Form)
Rev. Code Sec 5302.11

Know all Men by these Presents:

JAMES MITCHELL and JULIA E. MITCHELL (husband and wife) of LUCAS

County, State of Ohio , for valuable consideration paid, grant S to

ROBERTA B. CONN (widow and unmarried)
whose tax mailing address

is 1020 Lincoln Avenue, Toledo, Ohio 43607

the following real property

"Lot Number Two Hundred (200) in ENGLEWOOD, in the CITY of TOLEDO, LUCAS COUNTY, OHIO, said lot having a frontage of Fifty (50) feet on the North side of Lincoln Avenue and extending back between parallel lines a distance of Two Hundred (200) feet to an alley, as recorded in Volume 6 of Plats, Page 15."

(Premises known as 1020 Lincoln Avenue, Toledo, Ohio 43607.)

Subject to zoning ordinances, restrictions of record and public utility or other easements of record.
Prior instrument reference: Volume 1811 page 323

Witness our hand S this day of September 19 88

Signed, acknowledged and delivered

in the presence of

James Mitchell

Julia E. Mitchell

STATE OF OHIO LUCAS COUNTY, ss

The foregoing instrument was acknowledged before me this day of
September 19 88 by James Mitchell and Julia E. Mitchell (husband & wife)

Notary Public, State of Ohio

THIS SPACE FOR RECORDER'S USE ONLY

This instrument was prepared by
Kathleen W. Striggow, Attorney

4127 Monroe St., Toledo, Ohio 43606

Jim Mitchell is buried beside Julia in Woodlawn Cemetery in Toledo, Ohio.

Jim Mitchell's name has never been spoken on WWE television. He's not an inducted member of the Pro Wrestling Hall of Fame in Wichita Falls, Texas nor at the George Tragos/Lou Thesz Hall of Fame at the Dan Gable Museum in Waterloo, Iowa. Until recently, Mitchell had been largely forgotten in his hometown of Louisville and his adopted hometown of Toledo. Only a handful of diehard history buffs remembered his name.

Jim Mitchell may never be a familiar face to most wrestling fans, but his impact can be seen in every wrestling promotion that exists today. Mitchell was one of a handful of men who blazed a trail and opened the door for African Americans to become accepted not only in the ring but in the locker rooms. Alongside Jack Claybourne and Seelie Samara, he is arguably one of the most important African American wrestlers of the 1930s, 40s, and 50s, a man who helped blaze a trail for generations to come.

From the very beginning, and especially when he went on television, young dreamers were watching the Black Panther and finding inspiration for their future. Sweet Daddy Siki once shared his memories of Jim Mitchell with Greg Oliver. "I was born in Texas, but I was raised in Los Angeles. I remember when he started coming to California, I started watching wrestling. I was watching and I saw him wrestle. I thought it was pretty damn good. Even the Black Panther Jim Mitchell. I remember when I used to wrestle for the Sheik in Detroit, the Black Panther had a liquor store... I used to drop in to see [him] once in a while."

It was always Mitchell's hope that his success might inspire other African American youngsters to take up the sport of professional wrestling. Mitchell broke in during a difficult time for the sport, when attendance was down and payouts were small. That he was often the lone minority in the locker room did not make things any easier. But Mitchell persevered, and he hoped that others would follow in his footsteps.

"At the present there are about ten top-notch colored stars," he said in a 1952 interview with the *Baltimore Afro-American*. "And with the game continuing to grow in popularity, boys with the qualifications have the chance to make their presence known today much more easily than it was for 'Old Jim.'"

Mitchell's legacy carried on in Ricky Waldo and Bobo Brazil. It passed on to men like Luther Lindsey and Ernie Ladd and women like Sweet Georgia Brown, Kathleen Wimberly, and Babs Wingo. It continued with stars like Rocky Johnson, Abdullah the Butcher, Thunderbolt Patterson, Brickhouse Brown, Junkyard Dog, Tony Atlas, Koko B. Ware, Ron Simmons, Mark Henry, Booker T, Awesome Kong, Jacqueline Moore, and The Rock Dwayne Johnson. It continues today with top promotion stars like Jay Lethal, Big E, Kofi Kingston, Xavier Woods, Ricochet, Sasha Banks, Velveteen Dream, Lio Rush, Alicia Fox, ACH, Rich Swann, Cedric Alexander, and AR Fox as well as rising independent stars like Thomas Brewington, Desmond Xavier, Myron Reed, Mickey Muscles, Savannah Evans, Hy Zaya, Aja Perreira, Mr. Darius Carter, and the "Hitman for Hire" Mr. Grim.

Jim Mitchell broke down barriers in the hearts and minds of wrestlers and fans. He claimed his place as one of the top stars of the day through his exceptional work in the ring. He was a showman and a businessman. He was a husband and a father and a friend to many. He fought his way to the top of the world, gaining equal footing alongside wrestling's greatest star, Gorgeous George, and then, as "Brutal Bob" Evans advocates to all of today's aspiring wrestlers, he strove to leave the wrestling business a better place for those who came after him.

That's not to say the path he made was easy or even wide. For nearly four decades, aspiring African American athletes, male and female, faced the same obstacle that sent Ricky Waldo north of the border. Promoters of the day did not see black and white wrestlers, or any wrestler of color, as equals. Everybody had their African American guy, their Mexican, their Asian. Many promoters treated African Americans as special attractions, and the African American ladies doubly so.

This myopic view of black wrestlers was exemplified in a newspaper ad that appeared in South Carolina somewhere around 1976. A photo of Jim Mitchell was used in the ad to promote an appearance by another African American wrestler. The promoter either did not have a photo of the actual wrestler he had booked or didn't care to get one. One black wrestler was the same as another, hence Mitchell's photo was pulled out of a file and used to promote someone else. This is not the only incident I am aware of where Mitchell's face was used to promote another African American wrestler.

The gatekeepers to the business didn't make it any easier. In the January 1970 edition of The Ring Wrestling magazine, writer Crispus Whittaker spoke to one of the top African American ladies of the day (who declined to be named) about the women's situation in particular.

"The number one reason is the lack of adequate schooling for girls, white or black. Black gals come to me and ask where they can get wrestling training. I don't know where to send them." She goes on to state that she referred a number of women to a certain well-known (yet unnamed) trainer of lady wrestlers in South Carolina, but none of their letters were answered. African American men voiced a similar struggle at that time.

The lady wrestler interviewed goes on to talk about the pay differential for black women wrestlers. "The promoters think they can underpay Negro gals. They underpay the white ones, so they naturally believe they can get away with it in their dealings with the Negro women."

It wasn't just the lack of training and pay keeping potential new stars out of the business, of course. The interviewee also addressed the social pressures and challenges faced by young African American women in the wrestling business. "A Negro girl traveling alone, or even with another of her race, finds conditions far from ideal. The black woman will run into hotel trouble. She will find herself a loner socially. She will give it a fight for a while and then go back to waiting on tables or being a secretary."

Indeed, the racial tensions and Jim Crow laws in the South only added to the problems faced by African American wrestlers.

Bill Dundee once told me a story about checking into a whites only hotel and sneaking his African American tag partner in the back way. This wasn't the 1950s, but the 1970s!

Last but not least, African Americans who broke into the business were often cast in negative, racially insensitive roles, forced to play degrading stereotypes that would never fly today. African Americans knew that getting a spot on the card might mean playing an African savage, or a pimp, or a gang member.

Despite the lack of real opportunity for African American wrestlers, there was no shortage of African American fans who loved the sport. In fact the growing number of African American fans eventually led some promoters to give more opportunities to African American wrestlers. Sylvester Ritter, aka the Junkyard Dog, became one of the top stars in Bill Watts' Mid-South promotion largely due to the huge number of African American fans. Ritter was popular with fans of all races and rode that wave of popularity into a top spot with the WWF in the mid-1980s.

Wrestling became a place where racial barriers were broken outside the ring as well. The greatest example of this was Sputnik Monroe, a white wrestler who built a huge following with the African American fans in Memphis. Monroe became a regular at several African American hangouts in town and was arrested several times on charges of mopery and other bogus charges. Monroe hired an African American attorney to defend him in court, and the more he persisted with breaking the social mores of the time, the greater his popularity grew with the African American community.

Like many buildings in Memphis, the Ellis Auditorium, where Monroe wrestled, was segregated. Blacks had to sit in the balcony while whites sat in the seats down below. Monroe wasn't the only one who noticed that African American fans were being turned away from the sold out upper level while half the seats down below were empty, but he was the only person with the courage to do something about it. Monroe threatened to quit if the wrestling shows were not desegregated. Knowing that Monroe's absence would mean a devastating blow at the box office, the promoters eventually consented.

The Ellis Auditorium began selling out, and promoters of other sporting events took note. Soon they were desegregating their events, reaping the same financial benefits as the wrestling promoters.

One of the big questions I was asked when I first met Dave Marciniak was how someone like Jim Mitchell could have been lost to history. It took some digging for Dave and his girlfriend to learn much about him in the early 2000s, and the more they discovered, the more incredible it was that he could have been forgotten.

"I think he was blackballed," said Dave. "How else do you explain a guy just disappearing from history like that?"

The most likely answer to Dave's question is much simpler and less ominous. It's television. Mitchell was 42 years old before he ever appeared on television, and he was already on the decline. By the mid-1950s Bobo Brazil had supplanted him as the top African American star in the sport. It was the regional promoters who hyped Brazil as the man who broke the color barrier, the first true African American star in the sport. The heroes and legends of the pre-TV era faded into myth while the stars of the televised era became legends.

Not that Mitchell was forgotten completely. Like so many pre-television stars who, like Mitchell, deserve Hall of Fame status (Bull Curry, for instance), Mitchell became a cult favorite, folk hero to those who remembered him. When I first began sharing Mitchell's story online, a Twitter reader messaged me a story about his grandparents. "They loved Jim Mitchell. I still remember my grandma telling me, "That Ron Simmons is good, but he's no Black Panther!"

There's a vacant lot where the Carry-Out once stood, but the house on Lincoln Avenue still stands. All remnants of the Black Panther have been cataloged and sold off to various collectors around the world - save for the pipe collection, which still remains intact and in the possession of Dave Marciniak. Every item sold carries with it part of the story of this incredible man whose tale will be forgotten no longer.

Mitchell rarely spoke on the record about race, but in a 1951 interview with the Lynn Telegram-News, he expressed his gratitude for the way professional wrestling embraced him.

"Wrestling was the first [sport] to give the negro athlete a 100 percent equal opportunity. As a sport it pioneered in this respect. On my own experiences I advise boys of all faiths, color, and creed to enter wrestling if physically qualified, for that is the only thing that will count in a sport where ability is judged on its own merit in no way unsurpassed in any other form or endeavor."

Jim Mitchell wasn't the only Black Panther, but he was the original. He was a pioneer who blazed a trail for generations of African American athletes to follow. He remains a one-of-a-kind star who transcended race to become one of the most popular figures of his day.

ACKNOWLEDGEMENTS

First and foremost, credit needs to go to J Michael Kenyon, who was the first pro wrestling historian to respond to my inquiries for information on the Black Panther Jim Mitchell and started me down the rabbit hole. I miss his candor, his knowledge, and his guidance, and I wish he was around to read this book – after it's been thoroughly proofread, of course!

Second, thank you to Tom Burke, who has shared endless photos and information about Jim Mitchell with me over the years.

Thank you to Jerry Jaffe, aka Dr. Jerry Graham, Jr., and to "Flyin' Fred" Curry for sharing their personal memories of visiting Jim Mitchell at the Carry-Out.

Thank you to Jim Cornette who has pushed me to chase this story from the beginning and shared his own insights about the Black Panther's era. Thank you as well for making the connection with Mark Henry.

Special thanks to Mark Henry for his support of this project and providing the foreword for the book.

Thank you to Greg Oliver for sharing his Black Panther file with me, including the quotes from Sweet Daddy Siki and Jim Christy.

Thank you to Don Luce for sharing his story about Mitchell's lone appearance in Buffalo, New York.

Thank you to Abdul Alkalimat and Rubin Patterson, whose 2017 work *Black Toledo: A Documentary History of the African American Experience in Toledo, Ohio* provided a great backdrop for the Dorr Street community of Jim Mitchell's day.

A special thank you to Marcus Everett for going the extra mile to investigate the theory of the "mystery cards."

Thank you to the fans and neighbors of Jim Mitchell from Toledo who wrote in with their personal remembrances.

Thanks especially to Dave Marciniak for – intentionally or not – preserving so much of Jim Mitchell's story in letters, photos, and other artifacts found in Mitchell's former home.

Additional thanks for their assistance and knowledge goes to Koji Miyamoto, Tim Hornbaker, Ric Whitney, Bob Johnson, Bruce Hart, Timothy Johnson, Danny Daymon, Steve Ogilvie, Chris Parsons, Dan Westbrook, Kassius Ohno, Pat LaPrade, Sei Ozawa, Jimmy Wheeler, Scott Teal, K.K. Herzbrun, Randy Pease, Jason Freeman, Jason Campbell, Terry Sullivan, Wrestlingdata.com, the Pro Wrestling Historical Society Facebook group, and The Mothership Facebook group.

Thanks to Brian Last, Kenny Casanova, Jason Lindsey, and Tamaya Greenlee for their endless encouragement.

Thanks to Jessica, Lydia, and Sam for always supporting me. I couldn't do it without my family. Love you guys!

ABOUT THE AUTHOR

John Cosper is the founder of Eat Sleep Wrestle, LLC, and the author of numerous books about professional wrestling including the autobiographies of Dr. D David Schultz and Mad Man Pondo. He first discovered the Black Panther Jim Mitchell when writing his first wrestling book, *Bluegrass Brawlers: The Story of Professional Wrestling in Louisville*, and he's proud to finally bring this incredible story to light. John is also a screenwriter, science fiction writer, and children's ministry writer. He lives in Indiana, near Mitchell's hometown of Louisville, Kentucky, with his wife and kids.

ALSO AVAILABLE

Bluegrass Brawlers: The Story of Professional Wrestling in Louisville

Louisville's Greatest Show: The Story of the Allen Athletic Club

Don't Call Me Fake: The Real Story of Dr. D David Schultz
with Dr. D David Schultz

Memoirs of a Mad Man
with Mad Man Pondo

Lord Carlton: Aristocrat of the Mat
with K.K. Herzbrun

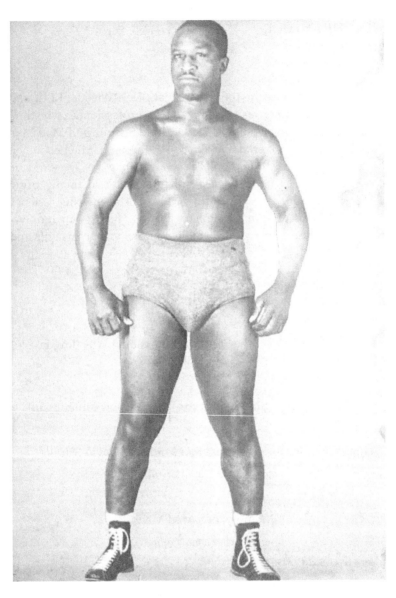

A favorite image of Mitchell's, he had this one blown up and framed in the house at 1020 Lincoln Avenue.

Made in the USA
Monee, IL
28 May 2020